COMMUNICATION
and INTERPERSONAL SKILLS

For health and social care

COMMUNICATION
and INTERPERSONAL SKILLS

For health and social care

MARGARET PORTCH

Hodder & Stoughton

A MEMBER OF THE HODDER HEADLINE GROUP

The characters and places in this text are fictional and any resemblance to actual people or places is entirely coincidental.

Copyright holders of photographs reproduced in this book:

- Format Photographers Ltd: pp 2 (*Maggie Murray*); 24, 65 (*Mo Wilson*); 33, 35, 90 (*Brenda Prince*); 87 (*Melanie Friend*); 97 (*Michael Ann Mullen*); 111 (*Jacky Chapman*); 116 (*Joanne O'Brien*); 138 (*Raissa Page*).
- John Birdsall Photography: pp 4, 10, 16, 19, 36, 41, 42, 43, 49, 63, 93.
- Photofusion: pp 26 (*Sarah Wyld*); 56, 78 (*Paul Baldesar*); 114 (*David Montford*); 115, 146 (*Gina Glover*); 118: (*Vicky White*); 123, 131 (*Crispin Hughes*).

British Library Cataloguing in Publication Data

Portch, Margaret
  Communication and Interpersonal Skills
  for Health and Social Care
  I. Title
  362.104256

ISBN 0 340 62085 4

First published 1995
Impression number   10 9 8 7 6 5 4 3 2 1
Year   1999 1998 1997 1996 1995

Typeset by Wearset, Boldon, Tyne and Wear.
Printed in Great Britain for Hodder & Stoughton Educational, a division of Hodder Headline plc, 338 Euston Road, London NW1 3BH by Bath Press Ltd, Avon.

This book is dedicated to Bob Cooke, with thanks for his understanding and support

CONTENTS

Introduction   ix

1 Developing communication skills   1
Non-verbal communication skills (NVC)   4
Listening skills   11
Summarising and giving feedback   14
Questions   15
Needs   18

2 Individuality and self-esteem needs   22
Individuality   22
Socialisation   25
Self-awareness   27
Self-esteem   30
Observing   33

3 Using communication and supportive skills   37
Showing warmth and interest   41
Communicating in groups   43
Evaluating supportive skills   51

4 Discrimination and its effects   62
Discrimination and stereotyping   62
Legislation relating to equality and opportunity   70

5 The care relationship   76
Support systems   76
Responses to care   79
Client rights and empowerment   80
Anti-discriminatory practice   81
Independence   81
Confidentiality   82

6 Taking part in discussions in care workplaces   85
Being clear   85
Checking information   90
Using the telephone   92

7 Skills in written communication   **97**
   CVs and job applications   98
   Memos   103
   Writing letters   103
   Log-book entries   108
   Reports   110
   Getting it write   111

8 Using images to communicate in care settings   **114**
   Ways of using images   114
   Designing posters and notices   116
   Diagrams, tables, graphs and charts   120

9 Reading and responding to information in care settings **130**
   Memos and letters   131
   Defining words   139
   Tables, graphs and diagrams   139

Further information   **144**

Bibliography   **148**

INTRODUCTION

Communicating with people and being able to provide support are central skills in any health or care job. This book is about those skills.

The information is aimed to interest students on health and care programmes, particularly people working towards gaining the GNVQ (Intermediate Level) in Health and Social Care.

The first three chapters are about how to develop skills in communicating and in providing support. Skills are described and explained, and plenty of helpful activities are included.

Chapter 4 covers discrimination and its effects, and chapter 5 looks at the care relationship and investigates issues of working with service users in health and social care.

The criteria for Unit 4 of the GNVQ in Health and Social Care at Intermediate Level are listed at the end of chapters 3, 4 and 5.

Chapters 6–9 are concerned with communication skills that workers need in care settings, including face-to-face, telephone, reading and writing skills. Activities are related to tasks normally carried out in health and care work.

GNVQ Core Skills in Communication at Level 1 are required for the GNVQ Foundation Level award in Health and Social Care. Core skills at Level 2 are needed for the Intermediate Level award. These skills are listed at the end of chapters 6–9.

The final chapter gives information about the National Vocational Qualifications (NVQs), which are available to voluntary or paid workers in Care, Child Care and Education and the Criminal Justice Services.

About the activities
The activities are highlighted in two ways.

? This type of activity usually asks you to think about something and write brief notes.

This type of activity suggests ways to try out practical skills in communication, through observing or communicating with others.

Both types of activity aim to help you develop your communication and interpersonal skills. They are often followed by comments which suggest possible answers or discuss what you may have learned – you will gain most from trying out the activities *before* reading the comments.

1 DEVELOPING COMMUNICATION SKILLS

> In this chapter, activities and information have been designed to develop your skills and knowledge about:
>
> - **Non-verbal communication**
> - **Listening**
> - **Questions**

If you are interested in care work you are probably interested in the way people think and feel. You are probably interested in how you can help people. You probably already *do* help people around you, even if you are not yet a care worker. Developing your communication skills will mean that you will become able to express your own thoughts and feelings more easily, and to help other people to say what they are thinking or feeling.

? ## ACTIVITY

- Think about a time when someone you know has talked to you about their feelings. Maybe it was one of your friends, a relative, a child or an older person. Maybe it was a baby, who could not talk, but showed you how he or she was feeling all the same.

- How did you react to the person? How do you think you may have helped him or her?

! ## COMMENT

You may have thought of quite a lot of examples. Whatever example you thought of, you probably remembered that you listened to the person. Maybe you asked them some questions? Maybe you said or did something to comfort them. Perhaps you looked interested or sympathetic.

All of these actions are ways of communicating supportively. In studying this subject you will be finding out how to increase your skills in listening, showing interest, asking questions, and showing respect for people, their personal beliefs and preferences. You will be able to appreciate their different needs which may be physical, social, emotional or intellectual needs, and to realise how these needs affect communication.

Emma and Pete

'But it's easy for you! You already know what you want to do after college,' wailed Emma.

Her friend Pete raised his eyebrows. 'So do you. Something with children, you said. You really like children.' He copied Emma's voice and grinned.

'Thanks! I don't sound anything like that actually,' Emma sniffed angrily. Then she smiled at the face Pete was making, trying to look sad and hurt.

'Oh, come on Pete, you know what I mean – you know you want to be a worker with elderly people. So it's obvious you've chosen the right course. But I've got no idea what sort of job I want.' She paused, staring thoughtfully into space.

'I do like the idea of working with children, but I want to do something where I can work with adults too.' She looked down and shrugged.

'What shall I do?' she asked.

Pete frowned and put a finger in his mouth. 'Hang on! I'm thinking!' Suddenly he jumped up with a huge smile. But he didn't say anything.

'Well? What?!' said Emma impatiently.

'Uh … I've forgotten …' Pete pretended to look puzzled, then, seeing Emma was still looking moody, he stopped joking and came to sit next to her.

'I suppose I'll think of something in the end,' she said.

'You're great with kids,' said Pete encouragingly. 'My mum says you're a great babysitter.'

'But I know your brothers, I've known them since they were really tiny. Care work you do as a proper job is different.'

....

Emma and Pete's story continues further on, but for now think about what Emma said last of all: 'Care work you do as a proper job is different.' It seems from what Pete said that Emma has the right kind of skills and interests for care work. His mother trusts her to look after Pete's younger brothers, and she enjoys being with people. So why does Emma think *working* in care would be different? One answer could be that she would be working with children (or adults) she did not know, at least at first. She would meet many different people, and would need to get to know them. As a worker she would have some responsibility, and people would rely on her to do her job, and expect her to have some knowledge and skills. So although Emma seems to be suited to care work, she is probably right to say, 'Care work you do as a proper job is different.' She will need to learn quite a lot and develop her skills. And so, of course, will Pete.

In Chapter 5, we will look at how the caring relationship differs from other types of relationship, at different kinds of support you can offer as a care worker, and at the different ways in which people respond to care.

Now look back at Emma and Pete's story, and try out the following activity.

? ACTIVITY

Emma and Pete were talking to each other. But how else did they communicate? Note down some examples of ways that Emma and Pete gave each other information about their feelings and ideas. (Clue: they did not just use words.)

! COMMENT

There were quite a lot of **non-verbal** messages in the story, and if you had been able to actually watch Emma and Pete, you would probably have noticed even more. Non-verbal messages are the messages people send to each other in conversation apart from the actual words they use. People communicate non-verbally in many ways. People's emotions are often shown through non-verbal messages, so you may be able to tell how they feel more from the non-verbal information you notice than from the words they use.

NON-VERBAL COMMUNICATION SKILLS (NVC)

People communicate non-verbally in many different ways. Some of these are:

- Eye contact
- Facial expressions
- Gestures
- Body movements
- Posture
- Use of space
- Touch
- Tone/emphasis/volume/speed of voice

Eye contact

People nearly always look at each other before they speak. They do this to see whether the other person is ready to listen to them. Once people have made eye contact it is much easier to start a conversation. So making eye contact is a signal to the other person that we want to speak to them, or perhaps to listen to them speaking. It is difficult to speak to someone who is not looking at us. If they are looking at someone else, we get the signal that they are either listening to the other person, or about to speak to them. If they have their back to us, we cannot make eye contact, so we have to move to a position where eye contact is possible.

Normal eye contact does not mean staring at someone – that can seem threatening. Normally, we glance at the person we are speaking to for a few seconds at a time, and during the conversation we keep glancing at them. These glances show we are interested and help us to check whether it is our turn to speak. When we are speaking, we continue to glance at the other person to check that they are listening. If someone is bored or distracted, they will often look away from us – so we can tell from their lack of eye contact that there is a problem.

SKILLS PRACTICE

Find a partner to work with, and try the following activities. You may find it useful to have a third person to observe and time your activities.

1   Sit opposite your partner, and try to keep constant eye contact with them. While you 'lock' your eyes with theirs, try discussing a subject such as your journey to college, or what you did yesterday. Keep in constant eye contact for at least one minute.

2   Now agree that one person will look at the other, while the other person looks away. Again, speak to each other for about a minute about something that interests you.

3   Finally, put your chairs 'back to back', and hold a conversation for about one minute.

Discuss with your partner how you both felt in all of these activities. If you had an observer working with you, get feedback from them also. Write some brief notes about how each of you felt during the activities.

COMMENT

Activity 1
People do not normally keep their eyes locked in constant contact in a conversation, so you may well have found this strange and threatening. Perhaps you found it very difficult not to look away?

In normal eye contact, people glance at each other for a few seconds at most, then look away, so it was probably difficult for you to talk or listen with your eyes locked on the other person's eyes.

Activity 2
Often people find that the person who is looking at their partner is the one who speaks the most. The person who was looking may have felt that the person looking away was bored or shy or uninterested. In normal eye contact, both people would glance at each other during a conversation.

The person who was looking away probably found this difficult, and probably also found it difficult to judge when to join in the conversation, because normally we look at the other person to see if it is our 'turn' to speak.

Activity 3

This activity sometimes gets quite noisy, because people who are not looking at each other and getting visual feedback find it hard to decide about volume. Also, because you are not making normal eye contact, it is hard to tell when to speak, so what often happens in this activity is that one person speaks while the other person ends up doing all the listening. Many people say they find this activity particularly uncomfortable, because they feel as if they are ignoring the other person, and not listening properly.

Sometimes in this activity people try to angle their heads as close together as possible, so that although they cannot make eye contact, they can show some interest and hear more easily. This activity also helps people to realise how much we often rely on being able to see the other person's mouth and lip movements when they are speaking. When we cannot do this, it seems strange and it becomes difficult to converse.

This activity helps you to understand how difficult it can be for a person in a chair or wheelchair to hear and listen properly to someone who speaks from behind them.

Facial expressions

When we look at another person we can see their facial expressions. People can signal many things through these. Small babies learn to make facial expressions partly by copying adults. Facial expressions show a person's feelings – we use our faces to show other people how we are feeling about them and what they are saying. We smile and laugh, raise our eyebrows to look questioning, draw down our eyebrows to frown or look angry or puzzled. Eyebrows, mouths and eyes are the main parts of the face that are used to form expressions. See how many different facial expressions you can draw just by changing the mouth and eyebrows on the faces opposite.

 SKILLS PRACTICE

With a partner, try the following activity.

- Use ten slips of paper, and write one of the following emotions on each slip: (1) Happy, (2) Sad, (3) Angry, (4) Worried, (5) Puzzled, (6) Surprised, (7) Depressed, (8) Furious, (9) Mischievous, (10) Horrified.

- Shuffle the slips of paper.

- One person observes, while the other person tries to make the facial expression that is suitable to the emotion on the slip of paper. The observer writes down the emotion they think they saw. The person making the expressions needs to keep a note of the order in which they made them.

- Now shuffle the slips of paper, swap roles, and repeat the process. Remember to keep a note of the order in which you made the expressions.

- Finally, compare notes.

! COMMENT

This activity probably helped you to realise that some emotions are easier to express and recognise than others. It may have left you realising that you have no idea what is happening on your face – mirror or video feedback can be useful if this is the case.

You probably also found that, as well as facial expressions, each person used a variety of non-verbal signals, such as posture, eye contact and body movements, to try to convey the emotion. This is an example of how non-verbal communication occurs in clusters – someone showing depression might look down, angle their head downwards, turn their mouth down, and droop their shoulders, for example.

Gestures and body movements

These are non-verbal signals people make, such as waving or nodding, shaking a fist or shaking their head. A shrug of the shoulders signals that the person does not know (or does not care) about something. Hand and arm movements are often used when someone is giving directions; try explaining the way to another person without moving your hands or arms! Some gestures, such as a 'thumbs up' sign, have special meanings and, like all non-verbal signals, these can vary from culture to culture.

Posture and use of space

Posture is the way a person sits or stands; this can give non-verbal messages. A person sitting up very straight with folded arms may seem alert and watchful. A person who is slumped with a drooping head may seem tired, bored or sad. The way we use space also gives messages – a person who sits as far as possible from others may seem nervous or unfriendly. A person who sits very close to others may give messages of friendliness and acceptance. On the other hand, if someone you do not know gets *too* close you may feel uncomfortable – you may feel that your 'personal space' has been invaded.

Touch

Touch is a powerful way of communicating non-verbally. It is an important part of loving relationships in families, and caring relationships between people. Love, care, comfort and validation can be shown through touch.

People may often be touched by care workers when physical care tasks are being undertaken – lifting, assistance with washing or eating, and other necessary tasks. It is important that these tasks are done in a way that sends positive messages of care and respect. Rough or hurried touch shows a lack of respect, sending uncaring messages. A carer needs to give their full attention to someone they are physically assisting.

Carers also need to be aware that touch can feel invasive, and that people differ in their feelings and reactions to touch. Putting your arm around someone who looks sad may feel like a comforting thing to do, but it may be inappropriate if you do not know them well. Messages sent and received through touch may also be affected by factors such as age, culture and gender.

SKILLS PRACTICE

With a partner, try the following:

- Write these words on slips of paper: (1) Interested, (2) Alert, (3) Relaxed, (4) Bored, (5) Anxious, (6) Tired, (7) Tense, (8) Afraid.

- Shuffle the pieces of paper, and see whether you can show the states listed using only gesture, body movements, posture and use of space. Remember to keep a note of the order in which you tried to show the states. (Try not to use facial expressions if possible.)

- Swap roles and repeat the activity.

- Compare your results.

COMMENT

This activity helps you to concentrate on how you use use your body to communicate. You may have found it difficult to show the difference between some states – between relaxed and bored, for example. This can help you to realise that sometimes when you feel relaxed you may come over to the other person as bored. Facial expressions help to show the difference, of course, but even so it is important to remember that these states can be difficult to tell apart. If you are trying to show interest and attention it is often useful to appear alert rather than relaxed.

Tone/emphasis/volume/speed of voice

It is not simply what a person says that matters – it is the *way* that they say it. If I say, 'I hope you'll be home by ten' in a gentle, quiet voice, it gives a very different message than if I say it in a loud, angry or sarcastic way. Putting emphasis on particular words also changes messages. 'What time did you get in last night?' '**What time** did you get in last night?' 'What time did **you** get in last night?' Each emphasis gives a different message to the listener and changes the meaning of the question. The way that people use tone, emphasis or volume makes a big difference to the meaning of the words they speak. Speaking quickly or slowly also makes a difference.

SKILLS PRACTICE

- Using the slips of paper from the 'facial expressions' exercise, try saying the following phrase to your partner: 'I wonder what we'll be having for dinner today?' (Remember to note the order you said them in.)

- Swap roles and repeat the activity.

- Compare results.

COMMENT

As you can see, this phrase can be used to show a wide variety of meanings and emotions by varying the tone, emphasis, volume and speed you use to say it.

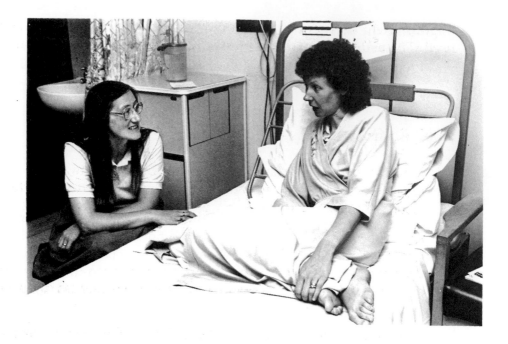

To show sadness or depression, you probably used a low tone and spoke slowly and quietly. To show happiness you probably spoke more quickly and varied your tone more. Anger may be shown by speaking either very loudly or very quietly, perhaps emphasising one or two words strongly; in this phrase emphasising 'we'll' or 'today' might have shown anger or indignation.

Clusters of behaviours

Non-verbal communication is not simple to understand, because people use a variety of NVC each time they speak or listen. NVC happens in **clusters**, so someone may smile, make eye contact and have an alert posture all at once, or may frown, look away and shrug their shoulders. These clusters help us to check exactly what the NVC means. Care workers use non-verbal communication to show interest in and attention to the people they are working with.

Clusters of non-verbal communication that show you are interested and attentive include making eye contact, smiling or having a sympathetic expression, nodding, adopting a suitable posture – which may be relaxed or alert, depending on what is being said – and speaking in a clear and friendly tone when you respond to the other person. All these signals can be used to encourage the person to speak to you, and to show that you think that what they have to say is important.

Care workers need to learn how to use non-verbal communication appropriately. Be aware that there are cultural variations in the way NVC is used. The activities that are suggested in this chapter will help you to develop your skills in this area.

LISTENING SKILLS

Listening is a skill that involves using non-verbal communication. An interested listener makes eye contact, nods and shows attention through their facial expressions and alert posture.

Listening to Duncan

Pete and his friends Phil and Duncan are in the canteen. Duncan looks depressed. The canteen is busy and noisy.

'Split up with my girlfriend last night,' says Duncan. Phil looks sympathetic. 'Pass the salt, can you?' he asks.

'She says I'm always too busy now I'm on this course. She's working, you see.'

Pete waves to Emma across the canteen. Phil is eating fast.

'I never have any money, and she's working, so she's loaded.'

'That's how it goes, eh?' Phil clatters his knife and fork on to his plate. 'I'm off to a film tonight. Want to come?'

Duncan looks sad.

'I've got no cash. Don't feel like it, anyway,' he sighs.

'Cheer up, mate! I split up with my girlfriend three times before we started getting on really well!'

Duncan gets up. 'Well, I'll see you then.' He walks away slowly.

Phil raises his eyebrows at Pete. 'What's up with him?'

Later, Pete goes round to Duncan's house. They talk in Duncan's room.

'Michelle wants to get out and enjoy herself after work, you see, Pete. She gets really bored in that supermarket.'

Pete nods. Duncan sighs.

'I always have college work to do. I'm not surprised she's bored with me.'

'You think she's bored with you?'

'Yeah. It's obvious. She said so, more or less. She said I didn't bother with her.'

'She thinks you don't bother with her?'

'Well, yes. She thinks I'm not interested. But it's just that I'm really busy with all this homework, and I can't ask her out if I haven't got any money, can I?'

'So she thinks you're not interested, but really you are?'

'Course I am.'

'Did you tell her that?'

'Well, not exactly. I thought she'd know. She must know I want to see her.'

'You sure?'

'Well … maybe I didn't say it to her … I thought she'd know.'

? ACTIVITY

In the first conversation Duncan did not really get listened to. Try noting down some of the problems you noticed about that conversation.

! COMMENT

You probably noticed that it was difficult for Phil and Pete to listen to Duncan in the busy and noisy canteen. Phil was trying to eat his lunch, and Pete was distracted when he saw Emma. Phil was trying to make Duncan feel better, but he did not really find out what had happened.

? ACTIVITY

The second conversation seemed more useful to Duncan. Note down why you think this was.

! COMMENT

Pete and Duncan had a quiet place in which to talk, where there were no interruptions. Pete tried to make sure he understood what Duncan was saying. He did not try to advise Duncan, or talk about himself or his own experiences.

? ACTIVITY

Remember some occasions when you have wanted someone to listen to you. Perhaps a time when you had a difficult day, or when you had an argument or a misunderstanding. Note down some of the things you wanted from the person who listened to you.

COMMENT

You may have said that you wanted time to talk and explain the difficulty. You might have wanted your listener to show interest and sympathy. You probably wanted them to understand what you were saying, and how you were feeling.

ACTIVITY

Now try noting down some of the things you *did not* want in that situation.

COMMENT

You probably did not want to have to rush what you were saying. You probably did not want your listener to talk a lot, or offer you a lot of advice. You probably did not want them to be busy doing something else while you were trying to talk.

Care workers use certain techniques that help them to listen without distracting the other person, and that helps the person they are listening to get their ideas and feelings clear.

Active listening

Care workers use certain techniques which help them to listen without distracting the other person; this helps the person get their ideas and feelings clear. This type of listening is often called **active listening** because the listener is not just hearing what is being said, but is actively *doing* things to encourage the other person. The carer is focusing on the other person, making eye-contact, nodding, showing interest, remembering what has been said and giving feedback. We may often use active listening with friends, but when using this skill as a care worker it is particularly important to remember to focus on the other person's needs.

Reflective listening

Pete used some **reflective listening** when he repeated parts of what Duncan had said. This encouraged Duncan to go on speaking, and also meant that Pete did not need to talk about his own views, as Phil had, but could concentrate on helping Duncan work out what he was thinking and feeling.

Reflecting back to the other person means repeating some of the person's own words, like a 'speaking' mirror. This can sound a bit mechanical if you use it too much.

Another way of reflecting back is to use **paraphrase**. This means to repeat the content of what the other person has said, but using different words. Paraphrasing also helps you to check if you have heard and understood properly, and it helps the other person to know whether you have understood them. It also helps them to clarify exactly what it is they are saying, because they have to listen to your paraphrase and work out whether that is what they meant to say.

SKILLS PRACTICE

It is useful to do these activities with two other people. You need one person to speak and one to observe, while you practise your listening skills.

You can swap roles, so you each get a chance to listen, and also to observe and give useful feedback to the person in the listening role.

Listening without speaking

- In this activity, the listener uses only NVC, and does not speak at all. They should concentrate on posture, eye contact and not fidgeting, and they may use nods, smiles, or other facial expressions.

- The observer should make some notes and give feedback to the listener.

Repetition and paraphrase

- In this activity, the listener aims to encourage the speaker to continue by **repeating** parts of what is said, and by **paraphrasing** (repeating the content of what is said using different words), which may also help the speaker to clarify their ideas.

- Get feedback from the observer.

SUMMARISING AND GIVING FEEDBACK

When you are listening to someone it is helpful to them if you can remember the main points of what has been said, and feed these back. Paraphrasing is one way of helping to get things clear, but it would take too much time to paraphrase all that is said. You may need to make a note of any action or issues which you and the speaker need to remember in a formal or work setting. When actively listening, however, it is useful if you can make a spoken summary of what has been said from time to time, and feed this back to the speaker. Summarising means picking out the main points that have been made and it gives an opportunity for you to check your understanding, as the speaker can comment on whether what you have fed back is what they meant.

Focusing on what is being said and occasionally summarising helps you to stay involved and interested, and helps the speaker to develop ideas. This feedback also helps the speaker to feel acknowledged and valued.

Be careful not to wait too long before summarising or you may lose the thread of what's being said. On the other hand, you don't want to put the speaker off by constantly interrupting to sum up. This skill takes some practice to develop.

SKILLS PRACTICE

This activity needs a speaker, listener and an observer. The listener should aim to show involvement and help get the main points of what is being said clear by stopping from time to time to feed back a summary of what has been said. The observer should watch and listen carefully and then give feedback to the listener.

SILENCE

Silence can be an important part of group or one-to-one interaction, when people are thinking, experiencing feelings or considering what has been said.

SKILLS PRACTICE

In a group, try sitting in silence for 5 minutes. Appoint one person to time the activity, observe and give feedback.

COMMENT

This activity enables you to focus on how you feel during silence. It is useful for you to consider this, because silences often happen in one-to-one listening situations or in groups. You may have felt calm and peaceful. You may have started to plan what you'll do this weekend. You may have made eye-contact or exchanged non-verbal signals with others. Five minutes of silence can seem a very long time, but as a listener or group leader, it is not necessary for you to interrupt a silence. In fact, it can be more useful for you to allow silences to continue, even if you do feel a bit uncomfortable with this at first.

QUESTIONS

Asking questions is an important part of conversation. It is a way of showing interest, and a way of getting to know another person. Sometimes particular information may be needed.

There are different types of question. Some types are:

- Open questions
- Closed questions
- Probes
- Prompts

Open questions

Open questions are questions that are broad, and give the person a lot of space to answer. An example would be: 'How do you feel about your course at college?'

Closed questions

Closed questions ask for more specific information. Examples would be: 'What course are you studying?', 'How old are you?' or 'Do you like music?'

Probes and prompts

These are short questions that build on other questions. A **probe** digs into an answer, aiming to get more in-depth information, and to get the person to think more about the subject. An example would be:

Open question: 'How do you feel about work?'
(Person answers that they enjoy some of their work but find much of it very stressful.)
Probe: 'What is it about your work that is stressful?'

A **prompt** aims to keep the person talking by suggesting a possible answer. An example of a prompt following an open question would be:

Open question: 'What sort of leisure activities do you enjoy?'
(Person answers that they like activities such as going to discos, dancing, keep fit and running.)
Prompt: 'You like being active?'

?

QUESTIONS QUIZ

Sort these questions into four types – open, closed, probe or prompt.

1   'Do you like apples?'
2   'Enjoy it?'
3   'How do you feel about college?'
4   'What parts don't you like?'
5   'What is your address?'
6   'What sorts of music do you enjoy?'
7   'Why did you do that?'
8   'Maths is your favourite subject?'
9   'Did you catch the bus here?'
10   'Can you tell me a bit about your past work experience?'
11   'Where was your last job?'
12   'Who is your doctor?'
13   'Have you thought about your career?'
14   'What ideas have you had about your career?'
15   'What kinds of games did you play when you were a child?'

For the answers to this quiz, see page 18.

?

ACTIVITY

Here is a list of questions. Imagine that you are talking to your college tutor for the first time. Write down how would you feel about answering the questions on this list.

- Very uncomfortable or angry

- Uncomfortable

- OK

'Where do you live?'
'Do you know other people on the course?'
'Do you have any care work experience?'
'What activities do you enjoy?'
'What type of placement would you prefer?'

'Do you get on well with your family?'
'Are you religious?'
'Do you have any problems with your travel arrangements for college?'
'Will you be having a hot meal at lunchtime?'
'Do you like canoeing?'
'Do you want to take Maths GCSE?'
'Are your parents married or divorced?'
'Who is your dentist?'
'What are your GCSE grades?'

! COMMENT

Questions can be **intrusive**. Some of the questions on the list would be very unsuitable for a tutor to ask at a first meeting. Some would be quite unnecesary. Some of the answers might be useful for the tutor to know, but the tutor might well lose your confidence and respect if they tried to ask you these before they had got to know you.

Even questions that might *seem* harmless, such as, 'Do you want to take Maths GCSE?' could make a person feel uncomfortable if, for example, they have tried Maths GCSE a few times and had difficulty with it.

If your tutor really *had* asked you all these questions at a first meeting, you might have felt you should answer, even though you were angry and uncomfortable. You might have thought that they would see you as awkward if you did not answer. This can happen in care settings, where a person may feel that they must answer questions, or that they risk being seen as 'difficult' if they do not.

It is important to be careful when asking questions, to avoid intrusiveness and to avoid making people feel uncomfortable or not respected. If you think that a question might be intrusive or make a person feel uncomfortable, think about *why* you are asking that question – do you need that information? How would you feel if the person asked you the same question.

NEEDS

Communication skills are useful to discover a person's needs. When you are able to assess a person's needs, you may begin to understand the problems they have regarding those needs.

We all have needs – for food, warmth and shelter, for love and security, for information and knowledge, for friends and relationships. The pattern of our needs changes over our life span; for a baby, food, warmth, love, attachment and nurturing are particularly important. For a young child, these are still important, but they also have, for example, a need for safe space to play and develop with encouragement from others. Adolescents need space to develop their individuality while having also the security of clear rules for behaviour. Adult needs include close relationships and employment. Elderly people may need physical help in order to perform certain tasks.

? ACTIVITY

- Try listing some of your own needs under the headings:

    Physical needs

    Social needs

    Emotional needs

    Intellectual needs

Try to show needs that are general – that is, that you think most people of your age or lifestyle might have – and needs that only you have.

An example of this might be:

Intellectual needs

General: Information
                 Knowledge

Specific: Information about renting flats (for moving out of home)
                 Knowledge about health and care services for career
                 development

- Compare your list with those of several other people.

COMMENT

You probably found that you have many different needs. When you compared your list with another person's you probably found that their specific needs were different from yours.

Your specific needs depend on your values and aims, on your experiences, beliefs and preferences. So, for example, though everyone needs knowledge, some people may specifically need knowledge on engineering to enable them to become an engineer, whilst others may need knowledge on babies and children. The knowledge people need may vary according to their age or circumstances.

Abraham Maslow suggested that as one need is satisfied, a person's aims, experience or preferences may change causing further needs. Maslow illustrates this idea in a pyramid rising from a base of physical and survival needs.

self-actualisation
needs: for self-fulfilment

aesthetic needs: to appreciate
art and beauty and to be creative

cognitive (intellectual) needs:
to know, understand, explore

esteem needs: to be competent, to be seen as
competent by others, and to be thought well of

love and belonging needs: to be loved and accepted, have
relationships and friendships, to belong

safety needs: to feel safe and secure, not to be in danger

physical and survival needs: food, water, warmth

MASLOW'S HIERARCHY OF NEEDS (MASLOW, 1954)

Further Reading: Gross, R. D. (1992) Psychology: The Science of Mind and Behaviour, *London: Hodder and Stoughton*

ACTIVITY

- Look back at your list of needs, and make a further list that shows how your needs are met. For example, your intellectual needs may be met by having conversations with friends, parents and tutors, by reading, watching TV or videos, using a CD-ROM, or attending classes at college.

- Are there some needs that you think are *not* fully met?

- Notice that *needs* are not necessarily the same as *wants*. For example, you might *need* physical warmth, and you might *want* to be on a warm, tropical beach. However, your need for warmth could be met by warm clothing rather than a sun-drenched holiday. A person who was abused as a child might want to stay away from other people to avoid getting hurt again – but they may still have needs for love and relationships with others.

Answers to questions quiz
Probe: 4, 7
Prompt: 2, 8
Open: 3, 6, 10, 14, 15
Closed: 1, 5, 9, 11, 12, 13

2 INDIVIDUALITY AND SELF-ESTEEM NEEDS

> This chapter looks at:
>
> - **Individuality**
>
> - **Respect, value and acceptance –
>   a non-judgemental approach**
>
> - **Developing self-awareness**
>
> - **Self-esteem**
>
> - **Observation skills**

INDIVIDUALITY

Emma and Pete

'Emma! Is that you?!!' Emma's friend Sarah staggered and pretended to look shocked.

Emma grinned. 'Yeah. Like it?'

'Like it? Wow, hang on! I mean, yes, of course I like it. It's really good!'

'Thought I'd change my image a bit. Now I've got some money from working on Saturdays, I can get my own clothes.'

'What did your mum say?'

Emma smiled. 'She's worse than me! She had on this weird kind of green sweater thing down to her knees, and purple leggings. She's going out on Friday, and she said, "You won't be wearing that jacket if you're baby-sitting on Friday, will you?" – like she might just want to borrow it, or something!'

Sarah was amazed. 'My mum'd go mad. She'd really like me to be wearing school uniform still.'

The bus arrived, and Emma and Sarah got on. Sarah looked sideways at Emma when they'd sat down.

'That, earring thing? I mean … doesn't it, kind of, hurt when you blow your nose … ?'

Emma giggled. 'It's a nose-stud, not an earring! It was agony, too, but I've got to do something to be different in our house. My mum's, like, still a "hippie", and Mark's really neat and tidy, kind of ultra-cool. I wanted to look like *me*.'

A voice from behind them on the bus called, 'Hi, Sarah! Who's your friend?' Emma and Sarah turned to see Pete, whose eyes widened when he recognised Emma.

At college, Pete and Emma met in the canteen at break-time.

'I can't get used to your new image Emma – it's really different.'

Pete stared at Emma as if he'd never seen her before.

Emma looked serious. 'I know it's "different" in a way, and I guess I did go a bit "over-the-top" trying to show I'm not like Mark or my mum. But it feels like me as well – the way I see myself. It's like I'm getting the idea of who I really am; not school uniform or hippie stuff my mum buys, but clothes *I* choose. And I used my own money, too – except my mum did just lend me a little bit …'

Pete looked down at his jeans and denim shirt. 'You've got a point.' He smiled. 'I want a leather jacket and those really black jeans. Can't afford it though. I'll just have to go on looking boring.'

Emma looked at him critically. 'You don't look boring. You look like you. But the leather jacket and black jeans idea is good, too.'

? ACTIVITY

Emma decided to express her sense of her own individuality by trying out some new clothes, a new 'image'. She wanted to show she was different from her family, a person in her own right. People differ in a variety of ways, not just in the way they dress. Try making a list of the ways people can be different from each other.

! COMMENT

You might have listed some of the following:

- Interests
- Beliefs

- Religions
- Cultures
- Things they enjoy/activities
- Abilities
- Ages
- Gender
- Physical appearance

One thing is certain: each person is unique – no-one is exactly like anyone else.

There are many things that influence the way our individuality develops. Look back at the story about Emma, and suggest some of the things that had an influence on the way Emma expressed her individuality.

The two main influences you might have noticed in the story were **money** and **family**. Emma had enough money to express herself through buying new clothes. Pete did not. Also Emma was influenced by her family in trying to look different from them, but she also knew that her mum accepted her individuality, and even wanted to borrow her jacket! This acceptance encouraged Emma to think it was OK to try out a new look and make her own choices. Sarah, on the other hand, did not think her mum would like her to look the way Emma looked.

There are many other things that influence the development of our individuality. The place we live in, friends and people around us, school, college and work, and the wider community and culture. We are also influenced by our beliefs, abilities, gender, age, religion and interests. All these affect the way we develop in to the unique person we become.

SOCIALISATION

Roles

As people grow and develop in society, they learn a variety of **roles**. They may learn the roles of daughter, son, worker or friend. They learn to take the role that 'fits' in a particular setting; at college, a person may be quiet or withdrawn, but in their family they may be confident and outgoing. At their part-time job they may be efficient and well-organised; when out with friends they may be carefree and fun-loving. People 'grow into' and learn roles, according to the different socialising influences on them in different areas of their lives, and in different groups they belong to.

Primary Socialisation

Socialisation in early life, as babies and children, is known as **primary socialisation**. At this period we are most strongly influenced by the behaviour and expectations of adults, family and carers around us. We learn roles and behaviour, beliefs and values that will influence our development as individuals, and that are the norms of the culture to which we and our family or carers belong.

As people grow older, they are influenced by their friends or **peer group** (friends and contemporaries), and by their education. These influences may sometimes conflict – that is, how things are done at school or college may be different from, and may not fit very well with, the ideas and values of a young person's peer group.

The process of socialisation continues throughout life.

Respect, value and acceptance

It is not clear in the story what Emma's mother thought of Emma's new image. She showed **acceptance** by admiring Emma's jacket and asking to borrow it. Sarah thought Emma looked 'really good', although she was curious about the nose-stud.

? ACTIVITY

- Remember a time when you chose something for yourself – it might have been clothes, music, a hairstyle, a new belief, or a new friendship, perhaps.

- How did you feel about what you had chosen?

- How did other people react to your choice?

! COMMENT

Perhaps not all the choices you have made have pleased the people around you. People are bound to disagree at times, or to feel that what you have chosen is not what they would want for themselves. Perhaps you can remember times when you have felt this about choices your friends or family have made. Care workers may not always agree with their clients' views or choices. They may not share the same beliefs, culture or religion. But this does not mean that one person is 'right' and the other 'wrong'. It is important for care workers to respect, value and accept their clients as unique individuals.

This type of respect and acceptance involves being **non-judgemental**. Each person has **values**: ideas about what they believe to be right or wrong. The values we hold are influenced by what is seen as normal in our culture (**norms**).

In a multicultural society these norms vary. Individual values vary depending on the different influences that have affected us as we develop. As we learn about different cultures and the different influences on people's development, we can learn to understand how it is that people have beliefs and values that are different from our own. We can learn to be open to differences, rather than being closed, defensive or judgemental.

This kind of openness to differences is an important quality for carers to develop. In the Further Information section (page 145), the **value-base** related to the **NVQ Awards in Care** is discussed. Openess to differences and a non-judgemental approach are part of the value-base that carers develop and practise when they work to NVQ standards.

SELF-AWARENESS

Emma and Pete

Emma was working on the computer in the IT centre. Pete stood behind her.

'Don't read the screen, Pete, I'm writing up my diary.'

'Really! Wow, let's see!'

Emma quickly flicked a switch so the text disappeared. 'Don't be nosey. It's private. Confidential. Top secret. And I hope I haven't lost it ... where's it gone?' She keyed in a command anxiously. 'What have I done now? What have I done, Pete?'

'Don't ask me. You're the genius with computers. I put the disk in upside down last week. Took ages to work out what I'd done.'

'It's OK, I've closed it properly now.' Emma retrieved her disk and shut down the computer.

'How come you're writing a diary? We haven't started our placements yet.'

'It's not about placements, it's about me. My life. It's a personal diary. We had to write about our lives for English, and I thought I'd keep on doing it.'

'What do you put?'

'I told you, it's secret.'

'Yeah, but what sort of things?'

'Well, just what I do. And things I'm thinking about. New ideas I've got. Problems and things.'

'What's it for?'

'Me. It's just for me, so I can read it. It's quite useful – it helps me work things out sometimes. I used to write a diary, but I stopped. Then I was trying to think what to do when I was practising typing, and I decided to do a diary.'

'Am I in it?'

'Typical man! Why should you be in it?'

'I'm not a typical man at all, actually. That's, um, stereotyping – we did that today, and what you've just said is a good example. I'm going to put it in my assignment …'

'OK. Typical irritating person, then.'

'That's better. Am I, though?'

'What?'

'In your diary?'

'I can't remember … you might be.'

'Typical woman.'

'Isn't *that* stereotyping?'

? ACTIVITY

What reasons did Emma give for writing her diary?

! COMMENT

Keeping a diary can be quite interesting. Care students in placement are usually asked to keep a diary or log of their activities, and the idea of this is that they can record what they did and how they felt about it, and use it to look back on their achievements and experiences, how they have developed and what they have learned in placement.

Emma decided to keep a diary about her life in general as well; she thought it would be interesting, and that it helped her to work out problems or ideas sometimes. Finding out about yourself is important in care work. If you know yourself well, and understand your own thoughts and emotions it can help you to understand other people. Knowing yourself is called **self-awareness**.

You might think everyone knows themselves; after all, we have lived with ourselves all our lives! But it is surprising how little time we take to think about what we ourselves are like – what we think and feel and *why* we think and feel things. Some people assume that everyone is basically the same, that we all have the same views and feel the same about things. But as we saw when we considered individuality, this is not true. People develop differently because, firstly, we are born **unique** and, secondly, we are **influenced** by many things as we grow up.

Developing self-awareness

Developing self-awareness can help us to understand what we ourselves are like, our particular strengths and interests, and we can think about what and who influenced us as we grew and developed. Emma's idea of keeping a diary is a good one, because although she is now 16 and at college, she is still growing and changing, meeting new people and learning new ideas. She will continue to change throughout her life. When we have learned to know ourselves well, this helps us to understand and 'empathise' with other people, to put ourselves in their position and see how life seems to them.

ACTIVITIES AND SKILLS PRACTICE

Keep a diary

This is a useful activity, because it can be done over a period of time, and helps you to gradually build up self-awareness, both through writing the diary and through looking back on what you have written.

Things you might write about in your diary:

- Activities/achievements
- Home
- College
- Placement
- Work
- Other people/relationships
- Problems
- Thoughts
- Feelings
- Things you have learned/understood

Autobiography (life story)

As Emma did for her English class, you can write your own autobiography. You can divide it in to chapters or sections that cover different ages or times in your life. You may have photographs or drawings that you can add.

Influences

If you have written an autobiography, or else just by thinking back over your life, try to work out what some of the influences on you have been. The following headings might be useful:

- Environments/places
- People – family, friends, teachers etc
- School/college/work
- Community
- Culture
- Religion
- Politics
- Abilities
- Gender
- Interests
- Activities
- Money

What influenced you in each of these areas as you grew up and developed?

Here and now

Take five or ten minutes now and then to get in touch with what you notice around you – what you can hear, see, and feel physically. What are you thinking? What are you feeling?

SELF-ESTEEM

Emma and Pete

Pete was looking worried. Emma sat down next to him and patted his hand.

'You OK? You look like you've just had a computing session,' she smiled.

Pete groaned. 'It's worse than that. I've got my placement. I've got to visit it. Tomorrow.'

'Well? So've I. I'm going to the hospital crèche. No earrings, no nose-studs, no high-heels, tell them more about your course,' she recited in a sing-song voice. 'I'm really looking forward to it.'

Pete groaned again. 'It's alright for you.' He looked away, and kicked the table moodily. 'I'm going to the hospital too. The Brent House Day Centre for elderly people. They'll hate me.'

'Oh, Pete, no, they won't. Of course they won't hate you. Why would they?'

'I don't know what to say to them. They'll think I'm useless. I don't know what I'm s'posed to do. I don't know anything.'

Emma patted Pete's hand again. 'That's not true, Pete. You're really interested in working with elderly people.'

'Yeah, but I don't know how to do it. They all know what they're doing. They don't want some total beginner getting in their way. What if someone collapses or something? What if I just sit there and say nothing? I can't think of anything to say. I don't think I can do it, Emma.'

'Did you say this to your tutor?'

'Nah, I just sat there. I didn't know what to say. I just agreed with everything. I'm s'posed to know what to do by now. She'd think I'm a total no-hoper if I said this.'

Emma hesitated. 'I'm not sure about that, Pete. I mean, none of us know much about it yet. And it's only a first visit, just to find out what they do, and meet people. No-one expects us to know the work yet. We've only been in college six weeks.'

Pete grunted dismally.

'Listen, Pete, it's OK to be nervous. Anyone might be. I don't know what the crèche'll be like. I'm just going to go and see. It's bound to be strange at first.'

Pete nodded.

'Isn't Salma going to your placement too?'

'Yeah. But she's got experience. She visits a lady in her flats. And she's really confident.'

'Why don't you arrange to meet her before you go in? It'd be easier if you were together. You could just listen, and get the hang of it all.'

Pete looked interested.

'She's over there. Shall I get her?'

'OK.'

Salma came back with Emma and sat down. 'Placement visit! At last!' she said cheerfully.

Pete looked uncomfortable.

'Ask her, Pete,' prompted Emma.

'Ask me what?'

Pete looked nervously at her. 'I wondered … I mean, I'm not sure … I wondered if it would be OK if we went to Brent House together tomorrow. I'm not sure what it'll be like.

Salma smiled. 'Fine, yes, of course, Pete. I went to Brent House with Mrs Patel once. She goes on Thursdays. It's really busy. I bet there'll be loads to do, when we start. Shall I meet you at the entrance, say, about ten to nine?'

Pete agreed with relief. 'Thanks, Salma, that'd be really good.'

? ACTIVITY

How would you describe Pete's general behaviour in this story? How do you think he was feeling about himself and his abilities? What non-verbal signs did he give about the way he was feeling?

! COMMENT

Even before Pete spoke, Emma had noticed he looked unhappy. He did not respond to her cheerful behaviour, so she realised he was seriously worried. He gave various non-verbal signs of his mood, such as looking away, groaning and kicking the table.

In this situation, Pete's self-esteem was low. He felt sure people would dislike him, and he felt unsure how to tackle the situation. He did not believe he would be able to do what was required, and he could not think of any way of sorting out the situation.

When a person's self-esteem is low, they may feel that they have no options. Pete is new to college, and he seems to be a shy and sensitive person. He has already had to meet many new people, and he has started to learn new skills. Although he made a joke of his difficulties with the computer, it may have worried him that he could not yet work out how to use the computers. He does not have money to buy the clothes he wants and look the way he would like to look. All these things may affect a person's self-esteem, and there are many other things that can also affect self-esteem.

People give both verbal and non-verbal messages about the level of their self-esteem. Pete was able to explain clearly what he was thinking and feeling, but not everyone can do this. Care workers use non-verbal signals to

help them work out how a person is feeling, and how confident a person is.

Salma was cheerful and confident. In this situation, her self-esteem seemed quite high. Care workers respond differently to people who have different self-esteem needs, by noting their verbal and non-verbal messages. A person who seems to have low self-esteem may need plenty of input, warmth and interest from the care worker. They may especially need to feel respected and valued, and to have their skills and strengths noticed.

Showing respect and value for other people involves noticing them as individuals, and responding to their particular individual needs. This is done both through careful listening, and through **observing** the other person: we notice things about them, listen to what they say, and show interest. As we get to know someone, we show we are interested in them and have noticed them as individuals by remembering things about them.

If someone tells us they are worried about taking an exam, we will probably ask them how it went, next time we see them. If, on the other hand, we totally forget what they said to us, they may feel that we are not interested in them. Care workers try to become skilled in observing people, listening to them and remembering things about them.

OBSERVING

True observation is a skill. We all notice things about other people, and sometimes we make assumptions about them, based on the way they look or speak, that may or may not turn out to be correct when we get to know them better. First impressions may or may not be accurate; skilled observation has to be done over a period of time.

? ACTIVITY

Find a place where you can watch other people – the library or canteen, for example. Make a list of the things you notice about the people around you.

! COMMENT

You probably included different types of non-verbal communication on your list. Even someone who is sitting on their own sends non-verbal messages through their posture, movements and appearance.

If you were watching people who were in groups, you probably listed many types of non-verbal signals that they sent each other.

If you could hear the people you were watching, you may have listed ways they spoke – tone, speed and volume. You may have listed some moods or emotions you guessed at from watching and listening to them.

Most of us have been watching and listening to people all our lives, so we hardly notice all the details that we take in. Often when we are talking to people we don't really take time to see all the non-verbal signals they give, because we are thinking about our own parts of the conversation, how we ourselves feel, and what we are going to say next. Practising observation of others is a useful way of becoming more aware of all their signals.

? ACTIVITY

In a public place such as the library or canteen, or even when watching TV, try using the following observer checklist to notice the details of communication between people. Try to watch and listen to two people or a small group in conversation for two or three minutes.

! COMMENT

Even in a short space of time there is a lot to comment on, especially if you are observing a group of people. You may find it quite difficult to keep track at first, but this gets easier with practice.

The things that you notice about people give you many clues about them. You can make guesses based on what you notice about how they may be feeling. But, of course, guesses can be wrong. Someone who is frowning and looking down may be angry, or they could be sad or puzzled or afraid.

It is important to **check out** your impressions. This can be done by listening to what the person says, and the way that they say it. Reflective

Observer checklist

Comment on:

- Facial expressions

- Eye contact

- Gestures and movements

- Posture

- Touch

- Clothes and appearance

- Speech – tone, volume, speed, emphasis

listening is useful here, because it allows you to concentrate on what the other person is saying and how they say it, and on their non-verbal communication.

You can also check your guesses and impressions by asking questions, but you have to be sensitive about how you do that. Questions can feel intrusive. It is important to check your impressions, but also important not to harass or embarass the other person. Usually it is best to notice things about people over a period of time, and to *gradually* check your assumptions.

If you are working in a care setting, you will have time to get to know people, and to get used to their particular ways of communicating. There is no need to rush this, or to try to find out everything about them the first time you meet them. You can show respect for people by taking the trouble to notice things about them, getting to know them slowly, listening to them, and checking your impressions over time. This process will show that you are interested in the person as an individual, and will help you to avoid making wrong assumptions about them.

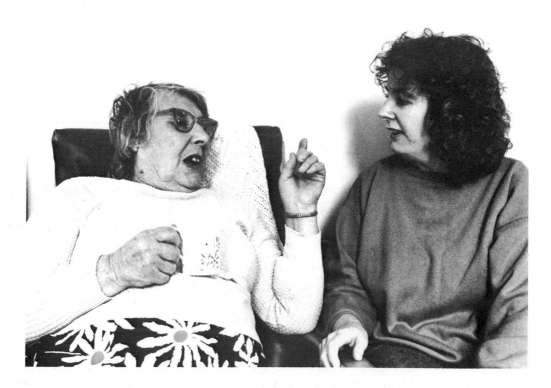

3 USING COMMUNICATION AND SUPPORTIVE SKILLS

This chapter looks at:

- **Using communication and supportive skills**
- **Showing warmth and interest**
- **Communicating in groups**
- **Evaluating supportive skills**

Pete and Emma

Pete, Salma and Emma were in the hospital canteen.

'How's it going, Emma?' asked Salma.

'Fine. Really busy today. We're making this giant frieze for one of the corridors. It's brilliant, I just get covered in paint. One of the nursery nurses has these pictures of African decorations on houses, and we've been showing the children. We're all just bathing in paint really!'

'We wouldn't have guessed – how did you get it in your hair, though?'

'Someone hugged me ! What colour is it?'

'Blue. Oh, and yellow near your ear.'

'That's OK – it goes with my shirt.'

Peter grinned. 'I've been in an art group this morning too! They started a new group today and they've asked me to go each week. I just watch and listen, really, and help with the paints and things. They asked me to explain to the group about being a student, and check if it was OK for me to help out. It was a bit nerve-wracking, but Mr Ranheim's there, that I was talking to last week, and he was showing me the pictures he did in the last group. He says he never knew he could paint until he came here.'

Salma looked thoughtful. 'It's strange I never thought about the elderly people doing art like that. I kind of thought they'd do bingo and jigsaws and things. They've asked me to go on a visit to the art gallery next week.'

Pete nodded, 'I'm going, too. They want a lot of helpers with people's wheelchairs. I'm pairing up with Mr Ranheim, because I've got to know him a bit. He's really interesting, and I think he knows I'm nervous, so he looks after me a bit.'

Salma smiled. 'That's what I didn't realise, either. I thought it was all going to be us looking after them, somehow. I didn't realise how much it would be about getting to know people, and them being interested in us; I was worried about how to push a wheelchair properly.'

Emma agreed. 'It's different from what you expect. The crèche is hard work, and sometimes I feel in the way a bit, because the staff all know what they're doing. But Mrs Burton said keep asking, and they'll tell me what they're doing and why, so that's what I do.' She looked at the canteen clock. 'Time to get back. See you later!'

Pete and Salma walked back together. 'Are you OK now, Pete? I know you felt pretty anxious at first.'

Pete nodded, 'Yes, thanks, I'm getting used to it. I like it here now. But I don't think I could have walked in the door the first day without you being there, looking really confident!'

Salma laughed. 'I wasn't really. But I'd been before, so I thought it would be OK.'

They reached the day centre, and went in.

In the afternoon, Pete and Salma were asked to mix in with people who were socialising in the day centre's coffee lounge. Pete sat near Mrs Hall, who came for the day from Holly Ward. Mrs Hall was quiet today; Pete wondered what he could say to her.

'Are you going on the gallery visit?' he asked at last.

Mrs Hall shook her head.

'No?'

There was no reply.

'Don't you want to go?'

Mrs Hall shook her head again.

'Don't you like art, then?'

'No, love.'

Pete felt a bit desperate. 'Er, can I get you some tea?' he asked.

'No, love. I've had mine.'

Pete felt as if Mrs Hall didn't want to speak to him. 'Er, I'll just get myself a tea, then,' he said.

Pete found Elaine Phillips, one of the centre staff, next to the tea table. 'How are you getting on, Pete?' she asked kindly.

Pete frowned. 'I was trying to chat to Mrs Hall, but she seems very quiet. She doesn't really know me, and I'm not sure if she wants to talk really.'

'She does seem worried today – I'll go and have a word, shall I?' suggested Elaine. 'You get your tea, Pete.'

Elaine went over to Mrs Hall and sat down. 'Hello, Mrs Hall, how are you?' She said.

'Oh, I'm alright, dear.'

'How are your sons getting on?' asked Elaine.

'They'll be alright, I suppose,' said Mrs Hall, she looked down, unsmiling.

'You said they'd been down to see you?' prompted Elaine.

'Oh, yes. They came on Saturday. Brought the children.' She spoke in a low, flat tone.

'That was nice, then?'

'Yes. But they've got their own lives, haven't they? They couldn't stay long. And the little ones get restless here, with nothing to do. It's not like when I was in my own place.'

Elaine nodded sympathetically. 'It must be difficult being away from your own things.'

Mrs Hall sighed, and hunched her shoulders. 'I can't go back. The doctor says I can't manage the stairs, and the doors are too narrow with this chair. They say I'll get one of those warden flats, but I don't know about that.'

Elaine nodded again. 'It must be hard to give up your own house, after all this time.'

Mrs Hall looked sad. 'Thirty-eight years I was there. The boys were still at school when we moved there. Not long after the war, it was.' She sighed again. 'I've heard those flats are pokey. And no privacy.'

'Well, it's not like your own house was, I suppose,' agreed Elaine. 'But the Anchor flats on Heathfield Road are quite nice – I know the warden there. Lovely gardens round them, too.'

Mrs Hall looked doubtful.

'Do you know when you might be going?' Elaine asked.

'No, dear. Maybe a few weeks, they said. I'm just waiting, now.'

'Well, I hope you'll hear soon. Once you've had a look round you might feel better.'

? ACTIVITY

- Pete noticed that Mrs Hall seemed quiet, but he had difficulty getting into conversation with her. Can you suggest some reasons why this might be?

- List Mrs Hall's NVC and suggest what it might show.

- What was different about the conversation Elaine had with Mrs Hall?

! COMMENT

Pete did not know Mrs Hall very well, so he could not very easily guess what might be a problem for her or how she might be feeling. He asked some 'closed' questions about a subject she did not have a lot of interest in. Also, she had some problems that were worrying her.

Elaine had had time to build up more of a relationship with Mrs Hall. She remembered things about her, and used these to get into conversation with her. She used prompts or reflective listening. This gave Mrs Hall a chance to discuss what was worrying her.

It is often not easy to help effectively until you get to know people you are working with. People often take time to build up trust and to feel comfortable with carers. Elaine showed that she was interested in Mrs Hall through remembering details about her family and situation. She used reflective listening to show that she had heard and understood what Mrs Hall said. She did not try to give advice or to 'cheer up' Mrs Hall, but she listened and showed that she understood, and that she respected Mrs Hall's feelings. By showing warmth and interest towards Mrs Hall, Elaine was able to provide some emotional support.

Emma, Pete and Salma were interested in each other's experiences, and were being supportive to each other. We show interest and warmth to friends because we care about them and want to know how they are feeling and what they are doing. We get support from our friends by sharing ideas and experiences with them, telling them about our difficulties and listening to their suggestions. It is unlikely that we will want to talk about ourselves to people who seem cold or bored; we do not tend to share problems with people who we think are uninterested.

SHOWING WARMTH AND INTEREST

? ACTIVITY

- Remember a time when you have shared a problem or difficulty with someone.

- How did you tell that person was **interested** in what you were saying?

- Did they show **warmth** towards you in any ways?

- Think about both what they actually said and their non-verbal communication.

Interest

Listening skills are important when we try to show **interest**. We will not seem interested if we are tired, distracted, busy or bored.

? ACTIVITY

- Remember some times when you have not wanted to listen to someone. Maybe in a class at school or college, maybe with friends or relatives, or at work.

- Can you remember how you may have shown non-verbally that you did not want to listen at that time?

- Perhaps you felt tired, and yawned or stretched? Perhaps you tried to look busy with something?

! COMMENT

Most commonly, people will tend not to make eye contact if they *do not* want to listen. They may look down or away. Sometimes people do this for other reasons, but it tends to signal lack of interest. If the person also yawns, we may think they are tired or bored. If their posture is very loose or relaxed, this may show lack of interest too.

Sometimes people fidget with things around them when they are not very interested or not ready to listen. Sometimes they are distracted by noise – it is difficult to listen in a noisy or busy place. Sometimes we might show we do not want to listen at present by busily doing something else, so that we do not seem approachable.

We can show interest by making eye contact, and by seeming alert, with an upright and not too relaxed posture. We need to make sure we are not fidgeting, perhaps by folding our hands in our laps. We need to choose a reasonably quiet and private place and not try to do another task at the same time.

It is difficult to listen and show interest if we are thinking about things that are happening in our own lives. We may have to decide to make a space for the other person; it is difficult to do this sometimes, and care workers have to make sure that they have people in their own lives who will listen to them, and show interest. If we do not have this, it is unlikely that we will be able to offer it to others. If we have friends who will listen to us, we can usually decide to clear our minds of our own problems at work, in order to be able to listen and show interest to people there.

We also show interest by **remembering** things about the other person asking them open questions, and using reflective listening, as Elaine did with Mrs Hall.

SKILLS PRACTICE

- With another person and an observer, practise showing interest through non-verbal signals as you listen to the speaker.

- Get feedback from the observer on your posture, eye contact, gestures and facial expressions.

COMMUNICATING IN GROUPS

Emma and Pete

Emma and Pete had been elected as group representatives by their class group. They had been to a meeting with the staff who taught on their course, and had been told that a group residential was planned. Emma and Pete had been asked to find out where the group would like to go and what they would be interested in doing.

They had been asked to bring suggestions back to the next meeting with staff. At a lunchtime meeting, attended by about half of the class, they asked for ideas and suggestions.

At first there was silence. Then a lot of people spoke at once:

'What about going to Spain?'

'How much money is there?'

'Do we *have* to go?'

'How do we get there?'

'I want to go canoeing.'

Emma put her hands over her ears. 'Not all at once! Hang on, everyone! Speak one at a time!' she shouted above the noise.

'How much money is there?' repeated Salma in the quiet that followed.

'Not enough to go abroad, we can choose something in Wales or the Lakes, say. The idea is a few days somewhere where we can all be together and do activities and do some work that'll count towards our course,' said Pete.

'How do we get there?' asked Phil.

'Minibuses. The college has some, or we might hire them. Depends when we go exactly,' Emma replied.

'Can we do canoeing?' asked Sarah.

'I think we can decide. It's up to us,' said Emma.

'When are we going?' asked Alan, a mature student. 'I'd have to think about how to manage, I can't leave Marie on her own with the children unless I've got time to make arrangements.'

Various people nodded and several started to speak.

Emma stood up and waved her notebook. 'Listen! Listen everyone. Let's organise this, or we'll get confused.'

'I'm confused now!' called Phil.

'Well, let's organise it like a proper meeting, then,' suggested Salma. 'We need a chairperson. I vote for Emma.'

'Is that OK?' asked Emma.

Alan looked at Pete. 'What about you, Pete?'

Pete smiled. He felt rather anxious in this situation. 'That's fine, Emma can be chair. Shall I write down what's suggested?' He reached for his notebook.

Emma sat down and looked round the group. 'OK, everyone?' People nodded.

'OK, what I suggest is that we go round the group, and everyone says what they want to do, and where. Then we can discuss each idea one by one.' She looked around 'Salma, you start.'

Salma suggested going to the Lakes. 'I've been there last year, it was brilliant. And you can do watersports and things. We had to make all our own food, we cooked outside one time.'

Pete wrote that down.

'What about you, Alan?' asked Emma.

'Wales. It's not too far, and we could go to the sea.'

'Sarah?'

'Anywhere with canoeing. I don't mind. But I'll have to ask my mum.'

'That's fine. They send out letters and forms for your parents to sign,' said Emma. 'Phil?'

Phil grinned. 'I vote for Spain! But the Lakes would be good, too. Lots of pubs!'

'What about you, Tariq?' asked Emma.

'I'd like to go to London,' said Tariq. 'We could visit places like Parliament and really look round.'

'Brilliant!' called Lisa. 'I vote for London too!'

'But we couldn't do canoeing in London,' objected Sarah.

'Yes we could, there's everything in London,' said Lisa eagerly.

'Order! Order!' shouted Emma. 'Some people haven't said what they want yet!'

The noise died down, and the group looked expectantly at those who had not yet spoken.

'I don't think I could go,' said Paula quietly, looking nervously round. 'I've got Jenny to look after, and she's at nursery, there's no-one to take her.'

Amanda agreed, 'My two are in the college crèche, I can't leave them, unless my mum could have them. I'd have to see.'

Emma nodded. 'Well, let's just think about where we could go, and note down that we have to think about childcare arrangements too, for some people.' Pete wrote busily.

'Where would you go if you could, Paula?' asked Emma.

'Well, Wales is nice. We went to Anglesey last year.'

'Amanda?'

'Anywhere, I don't mind. It'd be a holiday.'

Emma asked for views from each of the other members of the group. Finally they voted on the suggestions, and ended up with Wales as first choice and The Lakes as second.

'I'm not going if it isn't London,' said Lisa.

'Well, but most people want the countryside,' pointed out Alan.

'So?' Lisa frowned.

'Wales is really interesting, Lisa. And we could maybe visit London for a day another time,' suggested Pete.

Lisa shrugged and looked down.

'I don't mind Wales,' said Salma. 'Depends where exactly.'

'We need to check where there's places for residentials. Shall I talk to Mrs Brent and we could have another meeting to decide what we're doing?' suggested Emma.

The group agreed.

Alan's report

'The meeting was OK. Everyone spoke. I don't think they took enough notice of the childcare problems. Emma doesn't really understand about that because she hasn't got any responsibilities yet. I would have liked to chair the meeting myself, because I've done it for work lots of times. But Emma and Pete are the reps.'

Tariq's report

'I was glad the group got organised, I wouldn't have said anything otherwise. I don't think we discussed the different ideas enough, though. I still think London's a good idea. I'll go wherever most people choose, but I think it would have been better to ask people to think about the ideas and then have another meeting.'

Amanda's report

'I was in a rush because of needing to get the children from the crèche. I like the idea of the residential, but I hope we get more information so I can try to make arrangements. I don't really care *where* we go as long as I know when it is.'

Salma's report

'I thought the meeting went well. We got ourselves organised, and we came up with some ideas. It didn't take forever, so we had time to get lunch afterwards.'

Pete's report

'I felt very nervous in the meeting. I like being a rep, but I don't like talking in big groups, even though I'm getting to know the class now. I felt like I did something useful by taking notes. I felt angry when Alan suggested I should chair the meeting. I thought he'd have noticed by now I don't like doing that sort of thing.'

Lisa's report

'I thought the meeting was totally pointless. I wish I hadn't bothered going. As usual we just end up doing what Emma and Salma want. Next time I won't bother saying anything, because no-one listens.'

Sarah's report

'I thought the meeting was going to be a bit of a riot at first. It's difficult when there's no staff there. I'm glad I got a chance to suggest canoeing. I'm going to talk about it more at the next meeting.'

Phil's report

'I wanted my lunch! Don't know why everything always takes so long with that lot. All we need is somewhere next door to the pub. Preferably with a pool table. Hope no-one expects me to get in a canoe! No, I wouldn't mind it, really. As long as I don't have to get up too early!'

Paula's report

'I wasn't sure if everyone really listened properly. Most people just wanted to say what *they* thought. I thought it would have been useful to get more information on, say, two or three of the choices, and see what different facilities and activities were available. But no-one else seemed to think that, and I didn't want to argue.'

Emma's report

'I thought the meeting went OK, but I wish I'd thought about it more beforehand. Pete and I could have suggested how to organise it at the beginning, then. We didn't really plan enough. I don't think we had enough discussion. I didn't realise how much was involved. I think we should maybe talk about the different places we chose again, when we've got more Information.'

....

In this situation there were a lot of different needs and interests to take into account. Emma and Pete tried to organise the situation so that everyone could state their views. When a lot of people spoke at once, it was difficult to tell who wanted what, and the quieter people were unlikely to be heard.

Salma suggested the idea of a chairperson, which was accepted by the group. It was also useful to have someone taking notes, so people's ideas were not forgotten. By agreeing to speak one-by-one, the group made sure each person would be included, showing that they agreed to value each person's ideas. Even so, Lisa felt that her views had been disregarded. Pete suggested a way that her needs might also be met.

? ACTIVITY

- Think about group situations you have been in. You are probably involved in various different groups – perhaps a family group, a class group, a work group, or groups such as youth clubs, evening classes or sports groups or teams.

- Choose three different groups, and note down how you feel and behave in each group. Do you say a lot? Do you listen a lot? Do you take a leading role, or organise the group?

! COMMENT

People in each group vary, and each group has different needs. In one group you might do a lot of listening, but in another you might take a more organising or leading role.

It depends on what the group is for, who else is in it, how confident you feel in that situation, and what needs the group has that you can supply. On the other hand, if you are keen to organise, you might find ways of doing that in most groups you belong too. Or if you prefer to listen, you might do that in most groups you are in. It is useful to become aware of your behaviour in different groups.

Care workers are often in group situations – these may be formal groups, such as staff meetings, or case conferences with workers from other agencies and service users. Care workers may also be involved in helping to organise group activities, such as children's activities in a nursery, or leisure activities in a day centre, or a 'reminiscence group' with elderly people.

Communicating in these group situations is *different* from one-to-one communication. People have to take turns to speak, and this can be more difficult to do in a group than when there is only one other person to converse with. People may not always say what they really think in a group situation, or if the group is large some people may not speak at all.

Groups do not usually work well if the people in the group would rather not be there – people need to feel interested in the aims or task of the group for the group to work successfully.

SKILLS PRACTICE

When you are in group situations, try to observe how the people in the group communicate with each other.

- Is there a group leader?

- Do people mainly speak to the leader or organiser?

- Who speaks and who is silent?

- Do some people tend to 'dominate' the conversation?

- Do people 'take turns' to speak?

- What do you notice about people's non-verbal communication in group situations?

Encouraging participation in groups

People are more likely to want to take part in groups if they feel safe and secure, respected and valued. Group leaders or organisers need to make sure that the task of the group is clear to everyone, and that each person has a chance to state their views and ideas. Leaders also need to make sure that decisions are made and recorded. If only a few people get a chance to speak, or if there is not enough preparation or organisation, some people may feel left out or unsafe.

If disagreements arise, they can be discussed, and solutions can be found. Too much control of discussion or decisions by leaders may result in group members feeling powerless and uncommitted. This means that people may not do what was agreed in the group!

The group leaders or organisers need to check how the group meeting is progressing, and be aware of the needs of different individuals. Each person in the group has their own part to play in the group task. If only a few people speak, useful ideas and views will be lost, and this means the group task will not be done as well as it could be. Group members who talk too much should be encouraged to listen to the views of others. You might consider giving the task of making sure that everyone in the group gets heard to the most talkative group-member.

Groups may want to set standards for behaviour – this helps to avoid difficulties caused by aggressive, rude or critical behaviour, and encourages feelings of involvement and security. Aggressive or difficult behaviour can be challenged using these agreed rules, and the person can be encouraged to see how their approach is affecting others. A person who is aggressive or critical in a group may be feeling nervous, defensive or left out; their behaviour may harm the work of the group if not challenged.

Dividing into smaller working groups helps people to gain confidence and build relationships. Reporting back to the larger group then gives an opportunity for views to be heard by everyone.

Evaluating supportive skills

Emma and Pete

Emma, Pete and Phil were working in the Learning Resource Centre.

'What are you doing, Emma?' asked Pete.

'Evaluation sheet. You know, we had to make a list of ways carers could show interest and support, then make a tick chart to assess ourselves and each other.'

Emma smiled. 'My notes are a bit muddled, so I'm trying to get them sorted out first.' She shuffled a heap of papers.

'Those are your notes?' grinned Pete. 'I thought someone must have emptied a litter bin on the table …'

'Very funny. Mrs Brent says sarcasm is *not* supportive, actually. I suppose you've finished *your* evaluation sheet?'

'Not quite … I've written the heading, though … I'm just about to look in my well-organised file …' Pete tapped his file in a superior sort of way. Emma made a face at him and went on sorting out her notes.

Phil was leaning back in his chair. 'Finished mine ages ago. Can't find it now, though, so I may need to use your notes, Pete …' He looked innocently at Pete, who groaned.

'Am I the *only* person who writes things down properly?! You lot better get more organised soon … you'll need good notes for the tests.' He found his rough notebook and started to jot down ideas from his notes.

Phil looked at him. 'What sort of things are you putting, Pete?'

Pete looked up. 'Listen. You write some ideas, I'll write some, and Emma can write some. Then we can talk about them if you like.' He returned to his work.

'OK. Keep your hair on!' Phil found some paper and started to write.

Emma stacked her notes in a pile and sighed. 'I think I've got those straight now … There's one bit missing, though …' Her eye wandered to where Phil was working studiously. The paper he was using looked familiar.

'My notes on eye contact! Phil, you're writing on the back of my notes!'

Phil looked surprised. 'Sorry, so I am. Got any file paper?'

Emma grabbed her notes and stacked a pile of pages into her ring file, noisily snapping it shut. She then started to write busily. Phil stared around for a while, then rooted in his bag and found an old envelope, on which he wrote his ideas.

? **ACTIVITY**

- The rough drafts for assessment sheets that Phil, Pete and Emma made are shown on pages 54–55. The task was to include verbal and non-verbal behaviours that show warmth, interest and/or sincerity in a care setting. The assessment sheets were to be used to observe and assess each other's skills.

- Imagine you are marking Emma, Pete and Phil's work. How would you rate each rough draft? Try giving each draft a mark out of 25, and writing a few comments about the work. (Look back to earlier sections in the book to help you do this.)

! **COMMENT**

Phil's attempt was fairly basic! He did not explain *how* a person would 'look interested' or 'sound sincere'. Sitting *very close* might not be a good idea – it could be threatening, to some people – that is why it is important to notice individual needs. You might have given Phil's work about 5 out of 25.

Emma's draft was clearer, giving more details of the skills involved. She has left a few things out, but she has not added anything that is unsuitable. You might have given her draft 14 or 15 out of 25.

Pete's draft seemed to cover nearly all the skills you would be looking for at this level. He could have mentioned 'varying tone' and the idea of having an open and not defensive posture, but it is a very full skills checklist. You might have given it 22 or 23 marks out of 25.

? **ACTIVITY**

Make any additions you think are necessary to Pete's draft, then use the checklist to assess the following examples of one-to-one conversations in care settings.

Conversation 1 – In the lounge of a home for elderly people

Carer: 'Hello, Mrs Jones, can I talk to you for a few minutes?'

Mrs Jones: 'Well, I'm just waiting for my daughter – she'll be here in ten minutes …'

Carer: 'That's fine, ten minutes is fine, we needn't bother going to the office, let's talk here. Just a few things I need to check.'

Mrs Jones: 'Well …'

(Carer sits down next to Mrs Jones and gets out a pen and notepad.)

Carer: 'I didn't get your medical details, Mrs Jones; any pills, medicines, doctor's name?'

(She stops, and looks down at her notepad.)

Mrs Jones: 'What's that? I don't hear so well on that side – er – I don't think I know your name?'

Carer: 'I'm Jane Dobbs, you met me yesterday, I need your **medical details**.'
(Several people who are in the room look round as Jane raises her voice.)

Carer: (loudly) 'So, Mrs Jones, any **tablets** or **medicine**? **Doctor's name**?'
(Looks down at her notepad and taps it impatiently with her pen.)

Mrs Jones: 'I just need to get something from my room, my daughter's coming, you see ...'

(She gets up and walks out of the room.)

(Carer watches her walk away with a puzzled look.)

Conversation 2 – In the office at a young women's hostel

Care worker: 'Hello again, Susan – I'm Mary Cohen, I met you yesterday when you arrived.'

(Mary smiles and makes eye contact with Susan, who is a 16-year-old new resident.)

Susan: 'Hello' (She looks down.)

Care worker: 'I'm going to be your key worker while you are here, so I thought we could try to get to know each other a bit.'

(Susan still looks down, and doesn't reply, although she nods to show she's heard.)

Care worker: 'You told me yesterday you'd done some GCSEs at school and that you were planning to go to college.'

(Susan nods.)

Care worker: 'So maybe I can help you find out about college courses?'

Susan: (nods) 'OK, then.'

Care worker: 'Well, that's one thing we can do. How are you settling in to the hostel? Is your room alright? Do you have everything you need? Sometimes people want vegetarian meals, for example.'

Susan: (still looking down, mumbles) 'It's OK.'

Looks interested
Sounds sincere
Friendly
Doesn't keep nodding like one of those dogs in
the back of a car
Encouraging — asks things
Sits very close and makes eye-contact
Uses N.V.C.
Shakes hands

paraphrase
Active listening — focusing
summarising

Alert
- chooses a
  quiet and
  private place
  to listen

Non-verbal communication
   - smiles   - posture
   - nods   - gestures
   - eye contact

Not intrusive with questions
Uses open questions   - is not sarcastic
   and other types   - is not busy /
                                 distracted
Shows interest
Shows respect
Doesn't label people

In groups, gets people to join in
          gets them to take turns
          asks people for their views

Non verbal communication shows support and is appropriate.
- facial expressions
- posture (alert) - gestures
- position (not distant or too close)
- appropriate touch
- eye-contact - doesn't stare
   - doesn't avoid eye-contact

Uses active listening to show interest.
- NVC/eye-contact
- focusing/involvement
- remembers what is said
- summarises and gives feedback
- paraphrases/reflects back

Questions are appropriate and not intrusive.
- open   - probes
- closed   - prompts

Environment is appropriate.
- quiet
- private
- comfortable

Language used is appropriate.
- for age/understanding
- not sarcastic

Shows respect and validates others.

Takes account of people's beliefs and preferences.

Recognises and responds to different needs of others.
- physical
- intellectual
- emotional
- social

Does not show discriminatory behaviour.
- does not label or stereotype people
- recognises individuality
- is not prejudiced or judgmental

In groups
- encourages people to join in
- listens to views and ideas
- asks for views
- helps organise group where appropriate
- doesn't take over
- doesn't stay totally silent
- doesn't make fun of other group members

Pete

Care worker. 'Well, you tell me if there are any problems.'

(Susan nods.)

Care worker. 'Well, er, are there things you'd like to know, Susan?'

(Mary leans towards Susan, trying to make eye contact. Susan moves back in her chair, looking anxious.)

Susan: 'I'm OK. Only ...'

Care worker. (encouragingly) 'You're OK, only ... ?'

Susan: 'Can I use the phone?'

Care worker. 'Oh, yes, residents can use the pay phone at any reasonable time. It's in a little alcove just at the end of the hall. Mind you, it's very busy at times, so we ask residents to keep their calls as short as possible.'

Susan: 'I need to ring my friend.'

Care worker. 'That's fine. Well, then, Susan, there's a short meeting after tea for all residents, so I'll see you again then, shall I?'

(Susan nods.)

Care worker. 'We like residents to feel at home here. We think ...'

(The phone rings and she stops.)

'... I'd better answer that, just wait a moment, Susan.'

(Care worker speaks on the phone for a few minutes.)

Care worker. 'Well, Susan, sorry about that ... where were we?'

(There's a knock at the door, and the phone rings again.)

Care worker. 'I'll see you later on, shall I, Susan? After tea, at the meeting.'

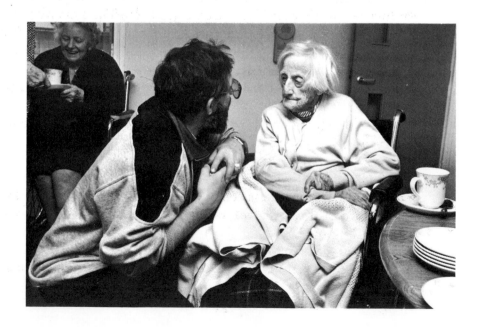

Conversation 3 – In the lounge of a home for the elderly

Care worker: 'Hello, Mr Bridges.' (Smiles and makes eye contact.)

Mr Bridges: 'Hello, Malcolm.'

Care worker: 'Did you say yesterday you wanted some help filling in a form, Mr Bridges?'

(He speaks directly to Mr Bridges, using eye contact, as he knows Mr Bridges has impaired hearing.)

Mr Bridges: 'I've got the form upstairs. Anyway, it's more private there, isn't it?'

Care worker: 'That's right. Or we can use the office if you'd like?'

Mr Bridges: 'I'm not going all the way down there. I'm an old man you know. I haven't got your young legs!'

(Care worker has offered a hand to Mr Bridges, who is frail and uses a walking stick. He assists Mr Bridges to rise, then waits for Mr Bridges to lead the way. They go up in the lift to reach Mr Bridges' floor.)

Mr Bridges: 'I don't know how I used to manage in that flat I was in, you know, Malcolm. It was all stairs. These lifts fairly take your breath away, they're that fast.'

(He is breathing heavily. Malcolm offers his arm, which Mr Bridges accepts.)

Care worker: 'Yes, it's a big help having a lift, isn't it?'

(They arrive at Mr Bridges' room. He unlocks the door and they go in – it's a bed-sitting room.)

Mr Bridges: 'I'll just get my breath, then I'll look for that form.'

(He sits down by the table. The care worker waits politely.)

Mr Bridges: 'Right, that's better. That's what I like about you, Malcolm, you're not forever rushing and hurrying. I can't stand it. That Martin, now, he can't stand still. I say – how can I think of anything with you jumping around? But he takes no notice, of course … doesn't matter what I say …'

Care worker: 'How d'you mean, "doesn't matter"?'

Mr Bridges: 'Ah, well, they're not bothered about you when you're old, are they?'

(He gets up slowly and starts to look for the form. He finds it and sits down. The careworker sits down also.)

Care worker: 'What's the form about, then?'

(He makes eye contact and looks alert.)

Mr Bridges: 'It's the opticians. They've that many forms now … I must have filled in two or three when I was last there, and now they've sent this through the post.'

(He passes the form to Malcolm.)

Care worker: 'Hmm. This is about eye tests is it? I think it's about getting free eye tests.'

Mr Bridges: 'Ah, well, I'm not supposed to pay.'

Care worker. 'Yes, that's it then … You don't have to pay, and you sign this and put the date here; they must have just forgotten to get it signed, maybe.'
(He smiles at Mr Bridges, and points to the place where the form needs filling in. Mr Bridges finds a pen and signs.)
Mr Bridges: 'Where's that envelope …?'
(He looks around and finds the envelope on the table. Malcolm waits while he does this, and while he slowly puts the form in the envelope.)
Mr Bridges: 'Pop that in the post box for me, Malcolm, when you go off, will you?'
Care worker. 'Alright then, Mr Bridges. I'm not off 'til five, though. Are you not in a rush with it?'
Mr Bridges: 'You don't rush at my age, son … Now, I'm staying here for a bit of a rest … You get on, I'm sure you're busy …'
Care worker. 'Alright then.'
(He picks up the envelope and makes eye contact with Mr Bridges.)
Care worker. 'I'll get this in the post on my way home. See you later on, Mr Bridges.'
Mr Bridges: 'Aye, see you, then. Thanks for your help.'
(Care worker leaves.)

! COMMENTS

Conversation 1

Not much interest or support here! The carer had mistakenly chosen a public place for a private and confidential conversation. She did not make eye contact, or introduce herself properly.

She did not know about Mrs Jones's hearing impairment, and when told about it she raised her voice, instead of changing her own position and speaking directly to Mrs Jones. This made the lack of privacy even more embarrassing for Mrs Jones.

The carer may have been able to show support by sitting next to Mrs Jones, but she did not smile or make eye contact, so support was not communicated. Interest was not shown, either – the carer only seemed interested in getting details for the records.

Conservation 2

The care worker in this conversation began well, smiling and making eye contact, introducing herself and using the other person's name.

She remembered what Susan had told her the day before, and offered some help.

But she also asked too many questions all at once, so that it was difficult for Susan to answer.

She encouraged Susan to speak, and gave information about the phone, but tended to label Susan as part of a group of residents.

Although the place was less public than in the first conversation, there were many interruptions towards the end. Speaking on the phone while Susan waited was likely to make Susan feel the worker wasn't interested in her.

Conversation 3
This conversation seemed to go well, with the worker showing warmth, interest and support.

The worker already knew Mr Bridges, which helped. He showed respect to Mr Bridges through verbal and non-verbal communication. He spoke directly to Mr Bridges, remembering that he had a hearing impairment.

The worker listened actively, and offered help with the form without 'taking over'.

The worker offered appropriate physical and emotional support. He was alert and sensitive to Mr Bridges' needs. He came over as friendly and sincere.

Assessing your communication and supportive skills

In order to develop their skills, people need to assess themselves from time to time, and to get feedback from others. When people are aiming to communicate well and be supportive it's important for them to find out how they are coming across to others. Being observed and assessed may be quite frightening, but everyone who has trained to help others has been through this – all health and care workers have to learn and practise their skills.

You can assess your skills by using tick charts or assessment sheets like the ones Emma, Phil and Pete thought up.

Feedback

Feedback from observers should be given in a friendly, supportive and positive way; it is difficult for people to respond to or learn from unfriendly feedback that is carelessly given. It is *never* appropriate to be sarcastic, make fun of people or put people down when giving feedback. It is most useful if feedback is about what the person said or did during the interaction, and what impresssion this gave the observer. Observers may also be able to make suggestions on how the person might develop their skills further, or may have relevant experience that would be helpful.

Making your own (honest!) self-assessment is very helpful, but you may still have difficulty knowing how you come across to others – you need to hear a variety of views.

Using video to gain feedback can also be useful. You can watch yourself interacting, and get a sense of 'distance' which is not otherwise possible. Some people find video feedback unnerving at first, but after a while it becomes more familiar to see yourself on screen; you can observe the reactions of others to your speech and behaviour in detail, and decide what is effective in your communication and what may need more development.

Audio-tapes can also provide very useful feedback for self-assessment. (N.B. see section on confidentiality if you are hoping to video or tape interactions involving service users in work or placement.)

Assessing the skills of others is helpful to you as well as them; it allows you to compare your skills with theirs, and to learn from them. Their difficulties or problems in interactions will help you learn just as much as observation of their successes.

When you assess yourself or others, it's necessary to have **criteria** – statements of the skills or knowledge to be achieved. The lists that Emma, Phil and Pete drew up were lists of criteria. One of the problems with Phil's list was that the criteria weren't clear – the person he was assessing wouldn't have known what to aim for, and Phil would not have had a clear idea of what he expected them to be able to do. A person reading Pete's list, on the other hand, would have a clear guide to the skills being assessed.

SELF CHECK
Chapters 1–3 concentrate on the skills and knowledge required in Element 4.1 of the GNVQ Intermediate Unit, Communication and Interpersonal Relationships. Look at the criteria and range outlined below and check that you have successfully covered all you need to know for this element.

GNVQ IN HEALTH AND SOCIAL CARE INTERMEDIATE LEVEL
UNIT 4   COMMUNICATION AND INTERPERSONAL RELATIONSHIPS

Element 4.1   Develop communication skills

Performance criteria

You must be able to do the following things.

- Explain why it is important for individuals, families, and groups to communicate.
- Demonstrate listening and responding skills to encourage communication with individuals in different contexts.
- Demonstrate observation skills to encourage communication with individuals in different contexts.
- Identify obstacles to effective communication.
- Evaluate your own communication skills and make suggestions for improvement.

Range

- **Importance of skills for:** development of self (intellectual, emotional, social), personal beliefs and preferences (culture, religion, politics, sexuality), development of groups/families.

- **Listening and responding skills:** facial expression, body language, eye contact, sensory contact, posture, minimal prompts, paraphrasing, summarising, questioning (open, closed), tone, pitch, pace of communication.

- **Contexts:** one-to-one, groups of three or more; peer groups, groups which include individuals of different status.

- **Obstacles:** environmental, social and cultural constraints.

- **Evaluate:** in terms of – self appraisal, feedback from others, suggesting improvements in methods.

DISCRIMINATION AND ITS EFFECTS

> This chapter gives information on:
>
> - **Discrimination**
> - **Legislation**
>
> The activities will help you to recognise discrimination and its effects on people.

DISCRIMINATION AND STEREOTPYING

The term 'discriminatory behaviour' means treating a person or a group differently from others. Usually, behaviour that is described as 'discrimination' refers to behaviour that treats a person or group differently in a negative, unfair or unjust way.

In the health and care sector, services are provided to meet people's needs. It is important that these services are provided in a way that is fair and just, and that does not discriminate against certain individuals or groups. This means that any person should have access to services, and should receive the same quality of service, as other users.

In terms of interpersonal relationships between health and care service users and service providers, it is important that people or groups are not discriminated against because of 'labels' that are applied to them

Each person is different and unique, whether they are a baby, a four-year-old, a ten-year-old, a young adult or an older person. Using labels such as 'the old folks' means that people are no longer being seen as invidividuals. Once we have labelled someone as 'one of the old ones' or 'one of the difficult ones', we tend to miss their individuality and only see part of what they are.

? ACTIVITY

Think about a group that you are part of – maybe your class group, or a social or cultural group, an age group or gender group.

Think of some of the **labels** you have heard used about this group.

Now think about the individuals in the group.

Think about how each person **differs** from the others.

! COMMENT

Although it may be possible, and sometimes convenient, to label people and
groups, it does not tell us much about people as individuals. Pete, Emma,
Salna, Phil, Sarah, Tariq and Duncan are all students in the same group.
They are all interested in care work, yet they are all very different as well. If
we link certain ideas or labels with the term 'students' and then expect them
to behave in certain ways because of this label, we are carrying out a process
called 'stereotyping'. This involves making assumptions about groups or
individuals which are not checked out, which become fixed ideas in our
minds, and which relate to fixed ideas in society.

Seeing an individual only in terms of their membership of a stereotyped
group means that their individuality is not being noticed or respected.

? ACTIVITY

What labels and ideas make up the stereotyped idea of a student?
    Is this stereotype true of any student you know?
    What labels and ideas make up the stereotyped idea of an elderly person?
    Is this stereotype true of any individual you know?
    Repeat this activity by looking at stereotypes of other groups, e.g. men,
women, 'disabled' people, teenagers, people who are unemployed, etc.
    Chapter 2 looked at the way in which an individual's development is
affected by social and cultural influences, and the need for a non-
judgemental openness to variety and difference was discussed. Negative
discrimination involves the opposite behaviour to such openness;

discrimination involves a judgemental and closed approach.

Ideas of what is seen as good or bad, valuables or valueless in society are often linked to power and lack of power. This can lead to groups being identified in terms of age, gender, race, or in other ways, and being seen as different, better or worse, more important or less important, than other groups. Attaching negative labels to factors such as old age or being female means that people who can be described as having that characteristic may be seen negatively, or as unimportant.

Negative discrimination occurs when people are treated less well than others because they have been identified or labelled as being part of a certain group.

Forms discrimination may take

Some forms of discrimination are:

- ageism,
- racism,
- sexism,
- discrimination on grounds of sexuality,
- discrimination on grounds of disability,
- discrimination on grounds of ill-health,
- discrimination on grounds of religion.

Ageism

This involves treating people in negative ways because of their age, such as advertising a job for someone who is 'young and fit', or treating older people as if they can't make decisions for themselves. This type of discrimination may devalue certain age-groups, such as children or elders, and involves the use of negative stereotypes of such groups, which may represent them as weak or powerless.

Racism

This form of discrimination usually refers to people being treated badly or unfairly because of characteristics such as skin colour, ethnicity or nationality.

A group that is attempting to be dominant in a society may try to exclude others by claiming that their own characteristics or ethnicity are 'better' than the characteristics or ethnicity of others.

Sexism

This terms describes discrimination based on gender.

In the past, a lot of sexism has been based on stereotypes of women's or

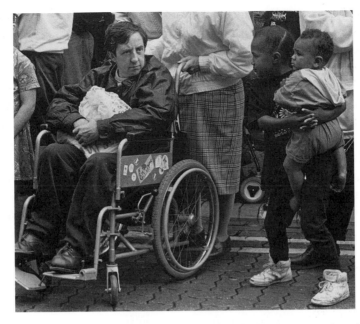

men's roles. For example, assumptions were made that mechanical or engineering tasks were more suited to men, while domestic tasks were more suited to women. Such assumptions were reinforced by social conditioning, that is, many people were brought up to believe these ideas were true, and may have felt they had 'learned' the truth of these ideas through experience.

A further problem was that many of the tasks thought appropriate for men were attributed higher status and often higher pay, whilst many of the tasks associated with women were given lower status, and less pay, or were not regarded as 'paid work' (child care and housework). As women and men came to be employed together in an increasing number of occupations, women were offered lower pay for doing the same job. This practice is now illegal. However, there are still differences in areas of employment, for example, many more nurses and nursery workers are women than are men, whereas the majority of doctors and solicitors (higher status and higher paid) are men.

Ability/disability

People may be discriminated against on grounds of physical or mental ability. A person who uses a wheelchair may be denied access to many places and activities because the environment has not been designed to include them or to cater for their specific needs. A student with a learning difficulty or learning disability may be denied access to her or his local college because it may be assumed that they will not be able to take part in college work or activities, when in fact the college does not provide a programme of learning suited to their needs, or support them in gaining access to learning programmes.

In these situations the individuals are labelled as 'disabled', but it is the actions and assumptions of service providers that are denying them access to provisions.

Health/Ill-Health

Discriminatory assumptions may be made about people who are physically or mentally ill. These assumptions sometimes include the idea that a person's illness makes them less able to make independent choices. In hospitals and care facilities, people may be discriminated against when they are not consulted or informed about their condition and treatment options. People with mental or physical health problems may experience discrimination in terms of reduced educational or employment opportunities.

Sexuality

Discrimination on grounds of sexuality occurs if a person is seen as less acceptable because of their sexual orientation. Sexuality may be described in a variety of ways including lesbian, gay, bisexual and heterosexual. Heterosexism is a term used to describe discrimination that defines being heterosexual as 'better' than other types of sexual orientation.

Religion

Discrimination on grounds of religion occurs when people are stereotyped in terms of their religion or denomination (group of people with specific religious beliefs). It may be assumed that people will behave in certain ways because of their religion, or it may be that one religion or religious denomination is seen as somehow superior to others. In health and care provisions, discrimination might be shown by not taking account of someone's religious beliefs or preferences, such as not providing facilities a person may need in order to practise their religion, or not catering for the dietary needs of people who hold certain religious beliefs.

Emma and Pete

Emma and Pete were walking into college. Pete kicked a stone into the gutter and frowned. 'I'm sick of hearing my dad's opinion about care work,' he muttered. 'He keeps going on about how it's not a proper job for men; he seems to think I'm a real wimp for wanting to do nursing. He says there's no money in it, it's women's work – and Mum just says don't take any notice of him.'

Emma nodded. 'It must be really annoying.'

'Yeah, it drives me mad the way he just does nothing in the house, leaves everything to Mum. The kids could starve to death or wreck the place as far as he's concerned – he just goes out to the garage and pretends it's nothing to do with him. If he has to baby-sit he rings Gran, and she comes round as if there's some sort of emergency! She won't even let me in the kitchen, she fusses around and tells me to go and watch TV and let her get on! It's ridiculous!' Pete glowered angrily.

Emma thought about what he'd said. 'I suppose your Gran never let your Dad help in the house, either – or never thought he should. That's how it used to be, though – I bet your Grandad thought 'a woman's place was in the home'?'

Pete groaned. 'He used to say, 'No wife of mine is going out to work. If the man of the house can't keep his wife and family, he's no right to call himself a man!' '

Emma laughed, then spoke sympathetically. 'Still, you've chosen a care course and you know people at college don't think like your Dad. Alec Johnson was a nurse before he was a lecturer, and Dave Goldberg's always talking about his children – he loves looking after them.'

'There are less men than women going for nursing though, aren't there?' said Pete moodily.

'Well, things take time to change,' suggested Emma. 'You're different from your Dad, and your Aunt Bridget's different from your Gran, too. She's at college, isn't she?'

'Yeah, she's doing Business Studies. Gran can't get over it. She says the children must be neglected, but they seem pretty cheerful to me – and Bridget just laughs, too. I suppose things *are* changing . . . '

? ACTIVITY

List some of the ways that men and women were seen as different in Pete's family.

What prejudices were shown by Pete's dad?

What effect did Pete's dad's opinions and behaviour have on Pete?

! COMMENT

In Pete's family, there had been a 'traditional' split between what was seen as women's work and what was seen as men's work. Women were seen as suited to work in the house and kitchen, and take responsibility for childcare, while men earned money outside the home to pay for the family's needs. Pete's grandparents seemed to think this was right and natural, and Pete's dad had been brought up to believe it.

Pete's dad seemed prejudiced about care work, seeing it as 'women's work' and not a suitable job for a man. He seemed prejudiced about childcare thinking the care of his younger children was a more suitable job for his mother than himself.

Pete reacted with anger and frustration to his dad's opinions and behaviour. He felt that his father saw him as a 'wimp' and he felt less confident about his career choice because of his dad's views.

Prejudices are often difficult to disentangle. Pete's dad's views were based on a mixture of things: his own parent's views and the way he had been brought up were very significant. When young people feel that their values, beliefs or way of life are challenged or threatened, they may become angry or defensive. Pete's career choice seemed to challenge his father's ideas and, rather than being open to change, Pete's dad seemed to feel he needed to attack Pete's choices. He supported his own beliefs by pointing out that nursing was a lower-paid occupation. He felt that it was 'women's work'. It's true that a lot more women than men are employed as nurses. Pete knew this, but he did not agree that this meant nursing must be more suited to women.

Discrimination and prejudice often have roots in history and tradition; there are many people with beliefs such as Pete's dad's even though things are changing. Many people are not aware of their own areas of prejudice and they communicate in a prejudiced way with their families and friends or at their workplace. Health and care workers need to be particularly self-aware in this area, to prevent any prejudices they may have from affecting the way they behave towards individuals or groups in the work setting.

Recognising our own prejudices is the first step towards becoming free of them. Once we have recognised a prejudice, we can take steps to find more information and views on the subject, allowing us to develop a more open and less judgmental or limited view.

Institutional discrimination refers to prejudices which are reinforced by organisations in society. Such organisations may include schools, colleges, local and central government, businesses and companies, public and private services, and the legal system.

Discriminatory practices can become part of the structure of such organisations so that some groups are excluded from gaining access to services or resources, or are treated unfairly, whether intentionally or unintentionally. Discrimination of this type by powerful organisations is likely to encourage the belief that such practices are sometimes 'part of life' or allowable.

Cultural discrimination refers to values and beliefs in society that reinforce prejudices. These may grow up through historical tradition and institutional practices, being reflected in uses of language, and perhaps being reinforced by the mass media.

Discrimination can be shown in various ways. These include:

- physical abuse

- verbal abuse

- threats

- devaluing

- avoidance

- exclusion

Discriminaton may be **direct** and overt (open and obvious), or may be **indirect** and covert (concealed). (See page 70.)

A person who is threatened, verbally abused or physically abused may suffer serious effects, such as shock, fear, distress, mental trauma or physical injury.

Forms of discrimination such as devaluing or undermining a person, or avoiding or excluding them, may have more gradual or less clearly seen effects, which are serious never-the-less. Self-esteem and confidence may be gradually worn down. A person who is continually prevented from gaining access to work or social life because they are in a wheelchair, for example, may grow to feel angry and frustrated, or powerless and dependent. A person who experiences the constant devaluing of their gender or sexuality may feel angry, isolated or alienated, or may begin to believe that they are not important.

? ACTIVITY

No-one is completely free from bias or prejudices. As a health or care worker, it's important for you to be self-aware, to know yourself well. This includes thinking about areas where you may be prejudiced.

You can consider this in two ways.

1. Think about how you interact with others. Are there some people you find it difficult to relate to, or who you avoid? What ideas, feelings or assumptions do you have about these people? Have you checked these?

   Do you behave or communicate differently with people from certain groups? How is your communication different?

2. Think back to the activity in which you explored the different influences on your development. Were there some influences that may have caused you to 'inherit' or develop prejudices, such as those Pete's father inherited?

Health and care service providers are often working with people who have experienced discrimination. Workers need to be aware of their use of language in order to avoid discrimination, labelling or stereotyping. They need to be aware of the self-esteem needs of service users, and to support people toward independence. Respecting and valuing people as individuals is an important part of anti-discriminatory practice.

Service users should be supported in making choices through encouragement of independence and guaranteed confidentiality. These areas of the service providers' role in the care relationship are described in more detail in chapter 5.

Most employers now have equal opportunities policies to support anti-discriminatory practice, and to make sure that service users' rights are upheld. In addition, there are laws and charters relating to the prevention of discrimination.

LEGISLATION RELATING TO EQUALITY AND OPPORTUNITY

Discrimination has been addressed in law by acts which have attempted to prevent discrimination on the basis of gender, race or disability. A major aim of legislation has been to prevent direct and indirect discrimination, and also to prevent victimisation of those who make or support complaints of discrimination.

In the Race Relations Act of 1976 and the Sex Discrimination Acts (1975 and 1986), **direct discrimination** was made illegal. Direct discrimination means treating a person less favourably than others would be treated in the same circumstances, because of their skin colour or ethnic background (Race Relations Act) or gender (Sex Discrimination Acts).

Indirect discrimination is also made illegal by these Acts. Indirect discrimination relates to setting conditions which exclude people unfairly on grounds of race or gender.

These Acts cover direct and indirect discrimination in the provision of services, such as health and care services.

The Race Relations Act of 1976 set up the Commission for Racial Equality. The CRE checks and monitors the way the act is working, and works towards the prevention of racial discrimination. It advises people who want to make complaints about racial discrimination.

The 1975 Sex Discrimination Act set up the Equal Opportunities Commission, which enforces the Act, as well as the Equal Pay Act (1970). The EOC carries out research and gives advice to employers, individuals or groups about sex discrimination, and about equal pay.

You can write to the Commission for Racial Equality and the Equal Opportunites Commission for information.

Their addresses are:

Commission for Racial Equality
10–12 Allington Street
London SW1E 5EH

Equal Opportunities Commission
Overseas House
Quay Street
Manchester M3 3HN

A summary follows of the Acts, Charters and Codes of Practice which aim to prevent discrimination.

The Race Relations Act 1976

- applies to England, Wales and Scotland (not to Northern Ireland)

- covers race discrimination in areas of:

  employment and training
  education
  housing
  the provision of goods and services
  advertising

- set up the Commission for Racial Equality

- relates to discrimination on racial grounds or against racial groups relating to colour, race, nationality, ethnic or national origin

- refers to direct discrimination, indirect discrimination and victimisation

Direct discrimination – where a person is treated less favourably than another person would be, on racial grounds. Direct racial discrimination is illegal whether or not it is intentional.

Indirect discrimination – where a racial group is disadvantaged by a requirement or condition which can't be justified apart from with reference to race.

Victimisation – where a person is treated less favourably than another peson would be because they have brought proceedings, given evidence or made allegations under the Act, or intend to do so.

The Sex Discrimination Act 1975, amended by The Sex Discrimination Act 1986

- covers discrimination in areas of

  employment and training
  education
  housing
  the provision of goods and services

- set up the Equal Opportunities Commission

- relates to discrimination on grounds of sex against women and men, and against married people with regard to employment and training

- refers to direct discrimination, indirect discrimination and victimisation

Direct discrimination – treating a person less favourably than another person solely on grounds of their sex. Sexual harassment (unwanted sexual attention) has been interpreted as direct discrimination under the Act.

Indirect discrimination – when a requirement or condition covers both sexes but in practice favours one sex because many or all of the other sex can't fulfil it.

Victimisation – where a person is treated less favourably for making a complaint or accusation, giving evidence or taking any action under the Act.

Other important legislation relating to health and social care

Name of Act	Dates	Key facts
Equal Pay Act	1970	In force from 1975, amended 1983
		Employees should have the same pay as others of the opposite sex for work that is the same or broadly similar
Disabled Persons (Employment) Acts	1944 & 1958	Employers should have 3% of their workforce as registered disabled, if they employ more than 20 people
Chronically Sick and Disabled Persons Act	1970	Provides for rights of access to public buildings, parking spaces and public toilets
		Local authorities must provide information about public services, and practical help in the home
	1976	Amended to cover access to places of employment
Disabled Persons Act	1981	Provides for rights of access to buildings as above, and also to travel on the roads
Disabled Persons (Services, Consultation and Representation) Act	1986	Provides for the rights of a disabled person or their carer to have an assessment of needs and be involved in care planning
National Health Service and Community Care Act	1990	To make the most of all opportunities for independent living for service users, ie; care in the community where possible
		To fully assess the needs of service users
		To introduce new funding methods, and make clear the responsibilities of the health and care services
The Children Act	1989	Sets out duties of local authorities and courts for many aspects of children's well-being
Mental Health Act	1983	Sets out powers of professionals in relation to those who, because of a mental disorder, are regarded as unable to make decisions about their own welfare
		Says that admission to hospital for treatment should be voluntary (informal) wherever possible

Charters, reports and codes of practice

These have been drawn up by the government, local authorities, and voluntary groups to set out needs and rights of people who use the services they provide. Some of the most important are set out below:

Charter or code of practice	Key facts
The Citizens' Charter	Gives performance targets for all public services, eg public transport
The Patient's charter	Gives performance criteria and targets for the NHS
	Gives complaints procedures for those who are not satisfied
Benefits Agency Customer Charter	Gives standards and targets for offices providing benefts
Royal Association for Disability and Rehabilitation (RADAR) 1991 policy statement	Says that disabled people have a right to live as and where they wish
	Says that disabled people know best what their own needs are, and should be involved in making their own support programmes
Declaration of Rights of people with HIV and AIDS	Restates rights of all UK citizens, but especially those with HIV and AIDS
	Includes rights to liberty, privacy and protection from discrimination
	Also includes basic rights to work, housing, food, a family, and education
Home life – a code of practice for residential care (1984)	Sets out important principles and good practice for those in residential care, similar to the NVQ value base
Community Life – a code of practice for community care (1990)	Recommended that there should be a charter for those using community care, similar to the more general Patient's Charter

GNVQ IN HEALTH AND SOCIAL CARE INTERMEDIATE LEVEL
UNIT 4 COMMUNICATION AND INTERPERSONAL RELATIONSHIPS

Element 4.2 Explore how interpersonal relationships may be affected by discriminatory behaviour

Performance criteria

You must be able to do the following things.

- Provide examples of the different forms which discrimination may take.
- Describe behaviours which may indicate discrimination.
- Describe how stereotyping individuals and groups can lead to discriminatory behaviour.
- Describe the possible effects of discrimination.
- Identify the rights which all individuals have under current equality of opportunity legislation.

Range

- **Discrimination based on:** age, disability, gender, health status, race, religion, sexuality.

- **Behaviours:** direct, indirect.

- **Effects:** short-term (anger, loss of feeling of self-worth), long-term (detrimental employment prospects, lack of motivation).

- **Equality of opportunity legislation:** relating to – gender, race, disability, pay, employment.

5 THE CARE RELATIONSHIP

This chapter helps the reader to recognise and understand:

- **Different kinds of support which make up an individual's support system**

- **Possible responses to professional care**

It also defines and discusses:

- **Client rights**

- **Anti-discriminatory practice**

- **Independence**

- **Confidentiality**

SUPPORT SYSTEMS

In everyday life, people develop different kinds of relationships with those around them. Society is a collection of inter-related and interdependent people; that is, each one of us depends to some extent on a variety of others, and each of us also supports others. We develop relationships and some of our needs are met through these. We also help to supply some of what other people need.

This is such a natural and everyday process that we may not normally think about it. We probably don't consider friends, family, teachers, carers, youth group leaders, religious leaders, doctors, clinic staff, neighbours, fellow workers or students as our 'support system'. We just interact with them, getting and giving support.

? ACTIVITY

To help think about what this idea means, you can draw a diagram or picture of your own relationships and contacts. Place yourself in the centre and show the people you normally relate to, or have contact with, around you. (You'll need quite a large sheet of paper to get a clear picture of this.)

! COMMENT

You may have been surprised to notice the many different people you relate to or have contact with. Some people may have seemed very important, while others were less central.

? ACTIVITY

Think back to the idea of needs, and try marking on the diagram what specific or general needs are met through support from the people you have shown, as well as specific and general needs *you* help meet for some of them by offering support.

! COMMENT

Some people may supply a lot of support to you, while others are only occasionally supportive in a particular way. Equally, you may support some people a lot, and others only a little or in one particular way.

There are probably some people who meet a variety of your needs – perhaps a member of your family or a friend supports you emotionally, socially and intellectually, by listening to your feelings or problems sympathetically, joining in social activities with you, and helping you with your studies. Perhaps you supply the same types of support to them, or to others.

Perhaps you show your doctor or dentist as meeting some of your physical needs. You may supply physical support to a relative. A parent probably supplies you with some financial support.

You may think at this point that you are part of quite a complicated support system. And each person relates to yet others to meet some of their needs, and also offers support to others.

Perhaps you notice a few gaps or areas where you don't get as much support as you feel you need. If this is so, you may want to think about how you can get the support you need in this area. Sometimes, gaps in our support systems may occur when a friend moves away or when we ourselves make a change in our lives, such as leaving school and going to college, or moving out of the family home. At such times, people may feel anxious, isolated or strange for a while, until they make new systems of support through meeting new people and making new friends. Change can feel uncomfortable for a while when this is taking place.

A lot of things affect the support systems people have. Some of these are:

- attitudes
- life experiences
- confidence
- beliefs and values
- self-esteem
- communication skills

- financial situation
- access to people and resources
- age

- physical mobility

- mental health

Support systems can be suddenly altered by major events:

- moving house
- accidents or illness
- retirement
- the birth of a child

- marriage
- loss or bereavement
- redundancy
- the breakdown of a relationship

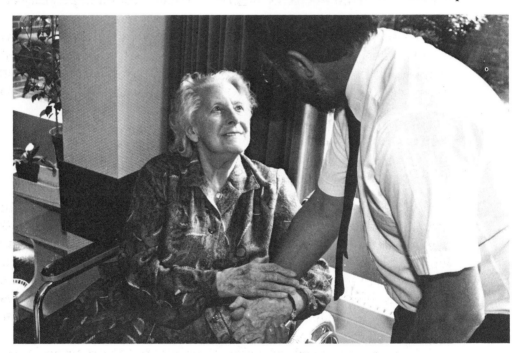

Most of us get some of the support we need from health or care services. Most of us are health or care service users or clients in some area of our lives. If our support systems break down suddenly or gradually in some way, we may need to use more services. We may have particular long-term needs requiring certain services, due to health conditions or frailty, loss or lessening of mobility, or learning difficulties, for example. Alternatively, we may have needs that require particular services for a short time to fill temporary gaps in our support systems.

? ACTIVITY

Look back at your diagram and use two colours to draw arrows showing

- support that you receive
- support that you offer

COMMENT

You may have found that there are some people you relate to where the arrows point both ways – each of you provides the other person with some support and each of you gets support (maybe meeting different needs) from the other person. There may be some people to whom you give support but who don't meet your needs, although you may feel that you gain a general feeling of pleasure and satisfaction from providing support to them. There may be others who meet your needs but who you don't provide support to – your doctor or dentist or teacher, for example, may come into this category.

This complicated pattern of giving and getting support and meeting needs changes over time and with changing circumstances. Society provides ways of filling gaps in support systems by setting up services and setting aside resources and funding to operate these. Health and care workers are the human part of these resources and services.

RESPONSES TO CARE

The professional caring relationship involves a worker or carer, who is usually paid to provide a service, and a service user or client. Whether or not the service user is paying for the service provided, there is an imbalance of power in these two roles. The carer has knowledge of services and systems that the service user may be new to; the service user may be physically dependent on the carer; the service user may be experiencing a crisis in his or her life, or a time of extreme emotional stress, whilst the carer is not.

Assessment of needs and care planning are the processes by which the needs of service users are clarified and met. These processes centrally involve the service user.

This does not mean, however, that the service user necessarily feels content or happy about their situation. A person may feel angry, resentful or afraid at having to discuss their needs with strangers, or at having to be cared for by people who are unfamiliar. If a need for care has come about through a sudden change in a person's life, they may be suffering the effects of loss or shock. If such a change has led to hospital or residential care admission, a person may be distressed and disorientated.

People in such stressful situations may react in various ways, including becoming silent or withdrawn, possibly depressed. They may feel angry and even act aggressively. They may feel confused and may find it difficult to express their thoughts or feelings to strangers.

These types of responses to care are not unusual and are

understandable. Most people would rather not be cared for by strangers and many of us do not like to accept help if we feel we cannot help or support others.

?   ACTIVITY

Look back at your diagram. How would you feel if all the arrows pointed to you, and none showed support you are able to offer to others?

How do you think you might act or behave if this was your situation?

!   COMMENT

Perhaps you would feel small and unneeded. You might feel that you are a burden on others. You might feel angry or resentful, or wish people would leave you alone. You would probably feel powerless and unhappy. Perhaps you would feel frustrated and bitter and find it hard to communicate.

Think back to the difficulties Pete experienced in discussing his work placement with his tutor (page 31). Pete had fears and uncertainties that he decided not to mention to his tutor because he thought these feelings would be unacceptable. We have seen how influences in society may 'encourage' us to behave in certain ways. As a male, and as a person in his particular family system, Pete had developed strong ideas that it was not acceptable for him to have fears and uncertainties or to discuss these. But he was able to admit his fears to Emma, whom he trusted and knew quite well.

In care realtionships, it takes time to build trust; sensitivity to others and strong interpersonal skills, especially as a listener, will help carers in this task.

CLIENT RIGHTS AND EMPOWERMENT

In care situations, service users have rights. These include people's legal rights and entitlements to equality of opportunity. Rights may be specifically listed in equal opportunity guidelines or charters of rights drawn up by particular organisations. The general principles of such guidelines and charters centre around people's rights to:

- freedom from discrimination (see page 62)
- respect
- independence and choice
- involvement in planning their care
- confidentiality

Empowerment of service users is the process of promoting rights so that people retain or gain power in their own lives. In the care relationship, the process of maintaining client rights and empowerment involves recognising individuality, offering respect, acceptance and a non-judgmental approach.

ANTI-DISCRIMINATORY PRACTICE

Carers need to be actively anti-discriminatory in their practice. This means being prepared to challenge discrimination and being actively involved in maintaining equality of opportunity. Self-awareness about your own behaviour is important so that you can ensure that you are not stereotyping or labelling people, or making assumptions about them.

You also need to be able to challenge discrimination from others. If you don't do this, you are giving messages that you accept their behaviour. Nevertheless, a challenge can be made sensitively, to enable people to learn and change their behaviour. For example, a child in a nursery who racially discriminates against another child needs to learn that this behaviour is unacceptable. However, they may often be repeating attitudes and behaviour learned elsewhere and will need your support and guidance to change. You cannot ignore their behaviour, because the child or children discriminated against need to be supported in maintaining their right to freedom from discrimination, which can affect their self-image and self-esteem. Children will learn from the way you behave so, if you act in a non-discriminatory and anti-discriminatory way, they can learn how to behave this way too.

To some extent, this is also true of adults; you can influence others by your appropriate behaviour.

If discrimination is built into the practices of an organisation, it may be hard to notice it at first. You need to be aware of the possible ways this can happen, for example, by thinking of groups or individuals who may be disadvantaged or excluded by the way a service is offered, or by noticing problems or lacks in the service. If you think some people are being excluded or disadvantaged, you should discuss this with your supervisor or other workers in order to decide what possible action you might take.

INDEPENDENCE

Being independent means acting for oneself and making one's own decisions. In care situations, it is important to promote independence, rather than to encourage or accept dependence. Promoting independence means allowing and supporting people to do things for themselves and to make their own decisions. A carer can assist in this by offering support without taking over a task, by listening to the service user and discussing their care with them. Independence can also be encouraged through involving service users in decision-making and in choices relating to their care. Showing respect for and interest in the other person helps them to maintain their self-esteem and feelings of personal power.

People who need physical assistance in toileting or other personal care such as bathing or dressing may already feel a sense of disempowerment or loss of independence through relying on another person to fulfil these needs. Ensuring privacy, being guided by the service user and checking that actions are meeting their needs is important.

Being well-organised, with practical needs thought about and provided for in advance, is a way of showing respect as well as being efficient. If two workers are involved in lifting or assisting a service user, their attention should be on the individual being assisted, involving and consulting them.

There are many types of equipment available to enable people to live more independently. Carers can help service users to assess the available equipment and to obtain and use the equipment most suited to their needs.

CONFIDENTIALITY

Information that is **confidential** is personal information that must be kept private. In care workplaces, all information about service users is private information; care workers should never discuss this information outside their workplace. Even within the workplace, it would not be appropriate for a carer to discuss a service user's business with others unless it is strictly necessary. Sometimes it *is* necessary for workers to share information with each other – the service user should always be informed of who will have access to information about them.

A worker or student on placement should make sure they understand the rules about confidentiality in the workplace. Always check this with a supervisor.

? ACTIVITY

Why do you think confidentiality is important in health and care work settings? Jot down as many ideas as possible.

! COMMENT

You may have listed points such as client's rights, need for privacy, importance of trust in care relationships, need for respect, hurt and damage that can result from lack of confidentiality. All of these points are reasons why confidentiality must be respected in care settings.

Service users have a right to privacy, and confidentiality of information is part of this. They have a right to be respected, and this is shown by respecting information they choose to give as confidential. Trust is needed between carer and service user that will be damaged if the carer discusses private information with others without the service user's knowledge. The service user may only choose to give information on the understanding that it is private, and the carer must respect that privacy. Also, it is usually simply unnecessary to discuss private information – such discussion must be regarded as unnecessary gossip or as a hurtful betrayal of trust.

However, there are some situations where difficulties may arise in keeping information confidential.

Firstly, a service user needs to be informed about what types of records are kept and who may have access to information. It is usually unrealistic for a worker to promise that no-one else will ever have access to information; for example, the point of record keeping is that important information about a person's care be available to those who are responsible for providing that care. The service user needs to know from the start that some others in the agency or organisation will be sharing in the provision of care and will have access to information if they need it. They should know, however, that *only* workers who need information will have access to it, and that they are also bound to keep information confidential.

However, most conversation is not recorded and does not need to be shared. Generally, a person should know what type of information is recorded and have access to it themselves – an atmosphere of distrust may build up in agencies where this is not the case.

A service user should be reassured that workers consult supervisors, and informed that this means the supervisor will also share information necessary to provide care.

Secondly, a service user needs to be assured that they will be consulted before any information is passed on to other agencies or any other person. This includes friends or relatives of the service user. It is up to the service user, not the carer, to decide what information may be passed on. If you are worried about a decision a service user makes about this, you should discuss the matter with your supervisor. If you are pressured for information by someone who feels they have right to know, you should also consult your supervisor.

In some very extreme situations you might need to override a request for confidentiality. This type of situation might be that a person is likely to take their own life or to harm others. Where a child is at risk, a request for confidentiality may also need to be overridden. However, even in these situations, only the information needed to provide necessary care or prevent harm should be passed on. In these extreme situations the reason for breaking the right to confidentiality is to protect the rights of others, including the rights of the carer themselves.

GNVQ IN HEALTH AND SOCIAL CARE INTERMEDIATE LEVEL
UNIT 4   COMMUNICATION AND INTERPERSONAL RELATIONSHIPS

Element 4.3 Investigate issues of working with clients in health and social care

Performance criteria

You must be able to do the following things.

- Describe how the caring relationship may differ in nature from other forms of relationship.
- Explain the ways in which clients may respond to being in receipt of care.
- Describe how different types of support may affect inter-personal relationships between clients and carers.
- Describe the role of effective interaction in caring relationships.
- Explain why confidentiality is of critical importance in health and social care settings.
- Explain the ethical issues which individuals may face in relation to maintaining confidentiality.

Range

- **Differ:** dependence of clients and carers, extent to which clients can be self-managing, perceived equality of relationship, perceived power, perceived knowledge and understanding about the situation.

- **Respond:** positive, negative.

- **Types of support:** information, social, financial, physical, emotional.

- **Role of effective interaction:** empowerment of the client, acknowledging individual's personal beliefs and identity, building self-esteem, building self-confidence.

- **Confidentiality:** client rights, client choice, building trust.

- **Ethical issues:** when request for confidentiality may need to be over-ridden, when another person pressurises the individual for information and the individual is uncertain whether they have a right to know, when action may need to be taken in the interests of the wider community.

6 TAKING PART IN DISCUSSIONS IN CARE WORKPLACES

Skills discussed in this chapter are:

- **Being clear when speaking**

- **Using relevant information when speaking**

- **Checking that you have understood what has been said**

- **Using the telephone:**
    taking messages
    planning calls

Other skills about taking part in conversations and discussions are covered in chapters 1 to 4. These include listening skills, and use of non-verbal communication.

In this chapter we will be looking at more skills related to face-to-face communication, and also at use of the phone in care workplaces. The GNVQ Communication Core Skills Elements 1.1 and 2.1 are listed at the end of the chapter. Some of the skills listed there have been covered in chapters 1 to 4, as they are part of the skills you need to provide emotional support.

BEING CLEAR

Emma and Pete

Emma was working on her Health Emergencies booklet. Pete was staring out of the window. Salma was reading.

'I wonder how they do that?' asked Pete dreamily.

'It's not too difficult if you've got the things you need,' replied Emma, underlining a heading in her booklet.

'No, I suppose not,' said Pete. He went on staring out of the window. 'I suppose if there's plenty of things lying about, it'd be easier.'

Emma frowned. 'A couple of nice, straight pieces of wood would be better, really.'

'Oh?' Pete looked as if he did not agree.

'Then you could join them firmly,' explained Emma.

'Is that what they do?' Pete looked puzzled. 'I'd have thought it was more like weaving, really.'

Emma sighed. 'Weaving? I don't think so. Straight pieces of wood joined firmly, and tested.' She searched in her pencil case for crayons. 'Salma, you've done one, haven't you?'

Salma looked up from her book slowly.

'Last week,' prompted Emma, 'you did one last week Salma, remember?'

'No, not last week – last year, it was. And I didn't finish it.' Salma looked back at her book. 'I didn't really need it then, but it'd be useful now,' she added.

'You've done one, have you, Salma?' Pete seemed surprised. 'What did you do one for?'

Salma looked up again. 'It was for a project on healthy eating'.

Pete gasped, 'Healthy eating! Really? But you can't *eat* them, can you?'

Emma looked up impatiently. 'Of course you can't! Salma, what are you talking about? You can't eat stretchers.'

'Stretchers!?' echoed Pete.

'Not stretchers, Emma!' laughed Salma. 'I'm talking about doing a survey. I did one last year on healthy eating – that's what *I'm* talking about – surveys.'

'What?!' said Pete, 'I thought we were talking about birds nests!'

....

Sometimes conversation can be very confusing! You might think that because you know what you mean, the other person understands as well. But this may not be true. Emma, Pete and Salma all thought they were talking about the same thing, but really they were all talking about something completely different. In this situation it did not really matter, but often it does.

? ACTIVITY

Try listing some situations where it would be important for people to understand each other.

! COMMENT

You might have suggested situations such as health emergencies or accidents, where people's lives might be in danger. In dangerous situations it is very important to give clear information or instructions, to check that people have understood you, and to check that you have understood what has been said to you.

Even when situations are not dangerous, it can still cause problems and waste time if people do not understand each other.

? ACTIVITY

The following example gives three ways of saying something. Which is the clearest?

- 'I didn't know what he meant, but I sort of thought, well, he'll think I'm stupid if I ask, so I kind of didn't like to ask, so I thought I wouldn't bother.'

- 'I didn't understand him, but I didn't like to check.'

- 'I didn't have the first idea what he was on about, but I thought, no way am I asking him and showing myself up, thank you very much.'

! COMMENT

In order to be clear, we have to think out what we say before we say it. This gets easier with practice. We also have to 'cut out' information that is not 'relevant', that does not *belong* in the particular story we are trying to tell.

? ## ACTIVITY

Try making a **clear** version of this muddled statement. Cut out information that does not seem to 'belong' in the story.

'I was on my way to Mrs Campbell's room because she said to me when she arrived yesterday, before I went off duty that was, but not just before because I did the log book afterwards and that took half-an-hour, anyway, she said she could do with some help in the morning, so I was going down there and as I was going past Mrs Jenkins' room – about 9.30 am it would have been, I think, because I remember noticing the postman coming up the drive out of the window so I knew the time.

'Anyway, Mrs Jenkins called me and said her laundry had come back muddled with someone else's, she wasn't too pleased. So I was going through it with her, and it *was* in a muddle, I don't know how that happened Mrs Jenkins, I said, because they're very careful normally, but it may have been with the machines going wrong after the power cut, and having to sort all that out, which doesn't usually happen, of course.

'So then, after I helped with that, I went on to Mrs Campbell's room, but I never actually got there, because when I was going through the lounge I suddenly saw this water on the floor, like, spreading, and I ran in the little kitchen because I knew the sink in there had been a bit funny the day before, but I couldn't see anything there, though. Anyway, Mr Crabtree was in the lounge by then, and he said, "That's a pipe burst, love." Well, he ought to know, he was a plumber for 47 years he was telling me yesterday, and so we both started trying to see where it was coming from, all that water.

'Mr Crabtree was saying it could be the bathroom pipe, so we were looking on the left of the room and then we noticed the radiator was cold. So Mr Crabtree said try looking along the radiator pipe and while I was doing that I noticed that book Mrs Jenkins lost two weeks ago fallen down behind the pipe, so that was a relief. She was amazed when I gave it to her, and she said the library fines are terrible now, so she was getting worried about it.'

'Anyway, the water wasn't coming out of the radiator, I don't know why that was off. Maybe Mrs Sproule switched it off, she likes to be cooler, but not everyone agrees, so there's been one or two arguments over it. It turned out to be the pipe from the little kitchen upstairs, and we got the water turned off and the plumber came and sorted it out, but it certainly caused some excitement, and I spent half an hour mopping up.'

We talk about things in different ways to different people. The way that we say things depends on how well we know the other person, and on what kind of 'role' we have in relation to them.

? ACTIVITY

The following statements were made by a student. Which statement do you think was made (1) to the student's friend, (2) to the student's college tutor, (3) to the student's work placement supervisor?

- 'I'm enjoying the placement, but I wish they wouldn't keep asking me to clean up the kitchen, I don't think I'm there to do that sort of thing. But I don't want to upset them by saying no.'

- 'It's really great, I've done loads of work with the residents, but they're always going on about cleaning that kitchen, like I'm a skivvy or something. No way!'

- 'I've really learned a lot through working here, I like talking with the residents especially. But I feel I sometimes get asked to do a lot of cleaning.'

! COMMENT

Care workers have to adjust the way that they say things to the needs of the person to whom they are speaking. Each person has different needs, which may vary according to their age, culture, gender, interests, physical and mental abilities, and other factors. Having respect for each person as an individual is important here. It would not be appropriate, for example, to speak to an elderly person in the same way as we would speak to a child.

SKILLS PRACTICE

With a partner, try the following exercises.

1   One person sits down, and the other person stands some way away. Begin to speak with each other. The person who is standing should walk slowly forwards until they cannot get any closer to the other person. Swap roles and repeat the exercise. Discuss how this felt.

2   One person sits down – this person is not allowed to move their head. The other person stands behind them. Try having a conversation in this position. Swap roles and repeat the exercise. Again, discuss how this felt.

3   One person sits at a low table with an activity, such as drawing a picture or doing a jigsaw. The other person stands next to them, and discusses their drawing or jigsaw with them. Swap roles and repeat the exercise. Discuss how this felt.

! COMMENT

People generally prefer to have space between them and the person they are speaking with. If you get too close, they may feel invaded or threatened. Also, it is physically difficult to speak with someone if you are having to crane your head back to look at them, and these discomforts will cause the conversation to be brief.

If a person has limited mobility, it is important to make sure that you position yourself so that they can see you and make eye contact with you when you are speaking with them. (This is also important when you are speaking with someone who has a hearing impairment.)

Generally, you should try to make sure that you are on the same physical level as the other person. If you 'stand over' someone who is seated, or who is smaller than you, they may find it threatening, and the conversation probably will not go very well.

CHECKING INFORMATION

Have you ever played a game where you whisper a message to the person next to you, then they whisper it to the next person, and so on round a group of people? What usually happens in this game, is that the original message gets shorter as it is passed on, until in the end it is very much shorter than it was to begin with. Usually important parts of the message get left out.

Sometimes people do not hear the whispered words correctly, and so they pass on what they *think* they heard, instead of the true message. The final version of the message is often very different from the original message. Try this activity out with a group of friends.

If you repeat the same activity, but allow each person to **check** the message with the person who whispers it to them, you will find that the message is passed around more accurately. Using this method, mistakes can be corrected as they happen. This second way of passing on messages does take a bit longer, but the message is less likely to be 'lost' or changed.

? ACTIVITY

It is important for people to make sure that they have understood what has been said to them. But sometimes people do not understand, and do not check the message. Suggest some reasons why people may *not* check?

! COMMENT

A person might be too embarassed to check. They might think that they are 'supposed to know', and that they will look foolish or stupid if they ask any questions. This is particularly likely when someone is a trainee or a student – they may feel that the 'trained' workers will be impatient or angry with them if they ask questions. They may feel that this would be seen as 'wasting time'.

When people are busy they may not take time to check information. Messages or instructions may be passed on in a rush, and people may not realise that they did not really understand the message until they try to act on it. By then it may be difficult to check what was meant.

Another reason for *not* checking might be that a person is not listening when the message or instruction is given. They might be thinking about something else, or be distracted by noise or activities going on around them.

In the long run, it is always best to check. Even if it seems embarassing at the time, it is better to check than to risk the difficulties and embarassment that may happen if a message or instruction has been misunderstood. A person who checks is more likely to be seen as careful and efficient than stupid.

Even when people are busy, it is best to check what has been said. Time is more likely to be wasted if the message has been misunderstood than if it had been checked in the first place.

Finally, although it is important to try to concentrate and listen properly, everyone fails to do this sometimes. If a message or instruction has been missed, it is important to ask for it to be repeated.

USING THE TELEPHONE

Most of us use the telephone to speak to friends and relatives. When we do this, we do not usually need to write down what we are going to say, and we do not usually write down what the other person says either.

It is the same as an ordinary conversation at work or college. If a student is chatting to their tutor in the canteen, they are unlikely to write down what the tutor is saying! But if the student is in a class, and the tutor is giving information about something, the student will probably take some notes. When people use the phone at work to make arrangements or take messages, they need to write things down.

Dealing with telephone calls

Different workplaces have different rules and procedures about phone calls. It is unlikely that a student in a workplace would be expected to answer the phone.

Whether you are a student on placement or an employee, you should make sure you know what the rules and procedures are about phone calls in your workplace. The same rules about privacy and confidentiality apply to phone conversations as to any other conversation you may have at work.

Taking telephone messages

When you answer the phone at work, you should give the name of the establishment and your own name, for example, 'Hello, Rowan Trees Hostel, Ceri Evans speaking.' When you do this, the caller knows they have got through to the right place.

Make sure that there is a pen and notepad beside the phone. When taking a message, ask for, and note down, the following information:

- The date and time of the call.
- The name of the person the message is for.
- The name of the caller.
- The phone number of the caller if a return call is asked for, and the suggested times for ringing back.
- The message.

As you can see, there is quite a lot to note down, so use a notepad that is large enough! Some workplaces have special 'telephone message' pads which have printed reminders of what to write down. Others have a special 'telephone messages' log book in which to write any messages.

? ACTIVITY

Imagine that you are a care worker in a busy workplace. How would you deal with the following calls? Write down what you would say, any messages you would take, and what further information you would ask the caller for (if any).

Call 1

'This is Renata Andrews, I'm Mrs Touati's daughter. Please tell my mother I'll be arriving at 2.30 today, instead of 3 o'clock as we'd arranged, because we'll be picking up my sister's children from school today. She needn't ring me back.'

Call 2

'This is Mark Lane, from Lane's Plumbers. We did an emergency repair on a pipe for you yesterday. We've now ordered the new pipe, but it won't be ready until next week. We could come and fit it next Thursday morning. Is that convenient? I was speaking to Mrs Jones at your place when I called before.'

Call 3

'This is Jane Simons at the Briggs Eye Clinic. I'm just ringing to say that Mr Patel is now due for his next appointment. Could Mr Patel ring me to arrange a time? I'm on 273 5373, I'll be here all day.'

Call 4

'This is Alan Knight at the Health Centre. Our computers are on the blink, and I've lost some of Mrs Smith's medical record. Could you look in her file and tell me her medical details please?'

COMMENT

The first message was fairly straightforward – you might have asked for the caller's number, just in case Mrs Touati wanted to ring back.

For the second call, you would have needed to ask for Lane's Plumbers' phone number, and for a more exact time than 'Thursday morning'.

The third call was clear and there was nothing you needed to ask – although in a real situation the caller might speak too fast, for example, and you might need to ask them to slow down or to repeat information, especially names and phone numbers.

In answering the last call you would need to think about privacy and confidentiality of information. You could offer to pass Mr Knight's request on to your supervisor, explaining that you are not allowed to give private information out over the phone. You could ask Mr Knight how urgent the problem is, so that you could inform your supervisor of that also.

Making telephone calls

It is easy to get muddled when making calls – the person at the other end of the line will not know what it is you want to say until you say it, and you may be afraid that you will forget something important. You can avoid this problem by writing down a plan before you make the call. Write a list of what you want to say, and of any questions you need to ask. You can tick off the points as you say them, and you can write down the person's answers as they are given. Although this may seem a lot of trouble, it is simpler and quicker than having to ring back because you forgot something. It is easier and saves time, because you do not have to try to think things out as you speak to the other person.

Planning a call

A plan for a phone call might look something like this:

- Ask to speak to Mrs Ahmed in the library services department. Introduce myself.
- Ask Mrs Ahmed whether a storyteller can visit the nursery next month for our *Eid* celebration.
- Suggest dates and times for the visit:
  Tuesday 15 March – morning or afternoon
  Wednesday 16 March – morning
  Thursday 17 March – afternoon
  Get exact date and time.
- Ask if she wants us to provide anything for her.
- Tell her there are 15 children aged between three and four, plus parents and workers.

- Ask if she will confirm the arrangement in a letter.
- Check that Mrs Ahmed has my name, the name/address of the nursery, and our phone number.

? ACTIVITY

Make plans that could be used for the following calls:

Call 1

The chiropodist is due to call at The Hollies, where you work as a care assistant. A full morning or afternoon will be needed, and the following days are possible: Thursday 20 May (morning or afternoon); Friday 21 May (morning); and Monday 24 May (morning). There are several people who would like to see the chiropodist, they are: Mrs James, Mrs Anwar, Mrs Mcpherson, and Mrs Lee. The chiropodist works from her home, her name is Ellen Granger. Your name is Chris Clark. Make a plan you could use to arrange the visit.

Call 2

You work in a nursery, and you have been asked to find out prices for some art materials that are needed. You want prices for 200 sheets of size A3 sugar paper (mixed colours); 200 size A4 thin card (mixed colours); 100 'chubby' wax crayons (mixed colours); 50 thick HB pencils; and twenty 500 centilitre tubs of poster paints, two each of yellow, red, light blue, green, black, purple, brown, orange, white, and dark blue. Your name is Jay Smith and the nursery is Green Park Nursery, St Benedict Avenue, Hopetown. You have been asked to get price quotations from Merry Times Ltd, and from Mr Johnson at Artstock Ltd. You would also like them to send you a list of all the stock they supply, with current prices.

GNVQ COMMUNICATION CORE SKILLS
LEVEL 1

Element 1.1 Take part in discussions

Performance criteria

You must be able to do the following things.

- Make contributions which are relevant to the subject and purpose.
- Make contributions in a way that is suited to the audience and situation.
- Confirm that you have understood the contributions of others.
- Make contributions which maintain the discussion.

Range

- **Subject**: straightforward.

- **Purpose**: to offer information, to obtain information, to exchange ideas.

- **Audience**: people familiar with the subject who know you.

- **Situation**: one-to-one, group.

LEVEL 2

Element 2.1   Take part in discussions

Performance criteria

You must be able to do the following things.

- Make contributions which are relevant to the subject and purpose.
- Make contributions in a way that is suited to the audience and situation.
- Confirm that you have understood the contributions of others.
- Make contributions which take forward the discussion.

Range

- **Subject**: straightforward.

- **Purpose**: to offer information, to obtain information, to exchange ideas.

- **Audience**: people familiar with the subject who know you, people familiar with the subject who do not know you.

- **Situation**: one-to-one, group.

7 SKILLS IN WRITTEN COMMUNICATION

This chapter looks at **writing skills** in care contexts, including:

- **CVs and job application forms**
- **Memos**
- **Formal letters**
- **Log-book entries and reports**
- **Organising writing and using correct punctuation**

Care workers need to be able to communicate in writing. They may need to fill in admission forms for new residents in a care home, or write brief progress reports about a child in a nursery. They may need to send memos to people in their own workplace, or write letters to people in other agencies. They may need to write in a log book, or to update records, perhaps using a word processor. The information care workers record is important, sometimes vital. It has to be written in a way that is clear and accurate, and that can be easily understood by others.

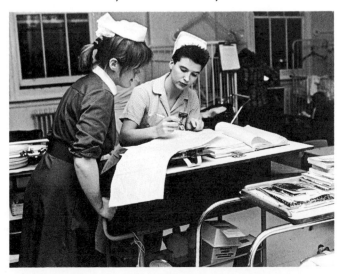

CVs AND JOB APPLICATIONS

To get a job in care work, a person must usually fill in an application form, or send a letter and a CV, which stands for 'curriculum vitae'. A CV is a list giving details about a person, including their qualifications, exam results, or experience that may help them to do the job they have applied for.

Here is Emma's CV.

CURRICULUM VITAE

Name: Emma Griffiths

Address: 52, Langham Hall Road, Oldford,
                 Merechester, MO3 2PL

Date of birth: 3:6:78

Education
1989–94 Merechester High School
1994–to date Central College, Merechester

Current course of study
GNVQ Intermediate Level, Health and Social Care (due to complete in July 1995)

Qualifications

GCSE	Grade	Date
English	D	July 1994
Maths	E	July 1994
Childcare	D	July 1994
Biology	E	July 1994

Work Experience
I have worked in a care placement at Merechester Hospital Crèche, helping with many tasks, including the general care of the children, and the running of the crèche. I have organised group activities for the children. I have also worked in a placement at the Oldford Adult Training Centre, helping to organise activities and supporting the service users. I regularly baby-sit for two boys aged three and five.

Interests
I enjoy swimming, and have a Silver Award for survival and a Bronze Award for life-saving. I am a class representative at college, which involves attending planning meetings with staff and organising meetings with students. I enjoy joining in group activities and I have contributed to the planning of a college residential weekend in Wales.

? **ACTIVITY**

Write out your own CV.

! **COMMENT**

Remember, it is very important to be **positive** about yourself on a CV – there is not a lot of space, and the employer or work placement supervisor who reads it will not know anything about you except what you write, so make sure you do yourself justice.

If you have a Record of Achievement, this will be very helpful in supplying the information you want for your CV.

Application forms

Often care workers apply for jobs on an application form. These can look quite complicated sometimes, but most of what is asked is fairly straightforward. (See the example overleaf of an application form that Anne-Marie Laski, who is a mature student, has filled in.)

For many jobs, you are asked to explain why you think you are suitable for the post. To explain why and how you are suitable, you need to look at the job description which is sent to you with the application form, and explain what experience you have that will help you do the tasks or take on the responsibilities in the job description.

It is important that what you say is related to the particular job you are hoping to get – a general statement about why you are suitable for care work is not enough.

The best way to tackle this is to write a sentence or two about what qualifications or experience you have for each task or responsibility listed on the job description. If you miss something out, the employer may think you do not have any knowledge or experience that would help you do that part of the job.

? **ACTIVITY**

Read the person specification on page 101 that was sent to Anne-Marie Laski, and then the statement that she wrote in the 'additional information' section of her application form.

Note which items on the person specification she has covered in her statement. Is there anything you feel she has left out?

APPLICATION FOR EMPLOYMENT

Post: Care Assistant

Please complete this form using black ink

Forename: Anne-Marie

Last name/surname: Laski

Address: 12, Walnut Avenue, Oldford,
Merechester MO2 3PK

Education (details of secondary education, giving dates and examinations passed)

Merechester High School	1970–75	CSE	French	2
			Maths	4
			English	3
			Science	5
Central College, Merechester	1993–to date	Currently completing GNVQ Intermediate Level Award in Health and Social Care		

Previous employment

Employer	*Post held*	*Dates*	*Reason for leaving*
Sparks Electrics, Merechester	Clerical Assistant	1975–78	To go full-time
Merechester Hospital	Clerical Assistant	1978–84	Started my family

Current employment
None. I am completing a course on 3 July 1994 (see above).

Names of two referees

Mrs K Brent
Central College
Merechester Road
Merechester MO3 7BG

Mrs L Diamond
Holly Trees Nursing Home
Holly Lane, Oldford
Merechester MO2 4PG

Signature of applicant: *A Laski*   Date: 10 June 1994

PERSON SPECIFICATION

Post: Care Assistant, Elderly Person's Home

Note to applicants: Please try to show in your application form, whether you meet these requirements.

Skills/Knowledge	Method of Assessment
1. To offer service users a high standard of care, having regard to their physical, emotional, intellectual, social and spiritual needs and taking account of their ethnic and cultural background.	Interview
2. To work as part of a staff team to meet service users' needs.	Interview
3. To observe record and seek advice on any changes in service users' well-being, condition or circumstances.	Interview
4. To liaise with agencies/service users' relatives as appropriate.	Interview
5. To ensure confidentiality and maintain safety and security in the facility.	Interview
6. To accompany service users to appropriate agencies, e.g. hospital, clinics, GP appointments.	Interview
7. To undertake domestic duties.	Interview
8. To work within the establishment's equal opportunities policy (copy attached).	Interview

Experience/Qualifications/Training	
1. To demonstrate an understanding of the needs of the client group.	Interview/Application form
2. To demonstrate ability to communicate with others in writing and face-to-face interactions.	Interview/Application form

Work Related Circumstances	
1. To be willing to participate in rotas, including some unsocial hours, on a flexible basis.	Interview
2. To be willing to participate in training.	Interview
3. To be willing to participate in meetings, including staff meetings, reviews and personal supervision.	Interview

Additional Information
(Please continue on a separate sheet if necessary.)

I am now completing a course leading to the GNVQ Award in Health and Social Care (Intermediate Level). I have achieved units in practical areas, such as providing support and dealing with health emergencies, as well as gaining a good knowledge of care provision and services and of the specific needs of elderly people. My work has been graded at Merit standard.

Recently I have worked in two placements with elderly people, firstly at the Holly Trees Nursing Home and then at Bret House Day Centre. I worked with teams of staff to help provide care for service users in each facility, giving physical help with mobility and at meal-times and joining in social activities with groups or individuals. I also did domestic work, including bed-making and laundry.

Some of the elderly people I have worked with have been frail or depressed and I have learned to be observant and sensitive to their needs, to listen and to use my communication skills both in day-to-day tasks and social activities.

I previously worked for six years as a clerical assistant at Merechester Hospital, keeping confidential records and helping with enquiries from patients, relatives and medical staff. I have learned basic information technology skills as part of my course and have gained units in IT, communication skills and numeracy.

I have worked with people of different ethnic and cultural backgrounds, both at college and on placement, and am aware of the importance of anti-discriminatory practice.

I very much enjoy working with elderly people and assisting them in maintaining independence and well-being.

COMMENT

Anne-Marie Laski's statement touched on most of the points covered in the person specification. She would be asked to give more details about her experience and knowledge at an inteview. She did not mention the items under *Work Related Circumstances* and would be asked about these. She would be expected to have read the attached equal opportunities policy and might be asked to give an example of anti-discriminatory practice, and/or how she would help an elderly person maintain independence in a residential setting. She might be asked in what situations she would seek advice from a supervisor, and to give examples of how she would contribute to maintaining safety and security in the facility.

Writing a positive and informative statement on an application form takes time and several drafts may be needed. Do not write straight on to the original, but rough out your ideas first. Use records of achievement and placement diaries to assist you and get a tutor at college, or perhaps one of your referees, to read the statement and give you feedback. Remember to keep a copy of what you wrote as you may be asked to give further details about your points at interview.

MEMOS

A memorandum (plural: memoranda, memo or memos for short) is a way of writing to someone who works in the same place as yourself. They are most often used in organisations that have different departments, such as schools, colleges, or hospitals.

A memorandum in a care workplace might look like this.

Memorandum

To: Jay Adams, Care Assistant   *From*: Nagina Bibi, Third Officer

Date: 15 May, 1994   *Subject*: Finance for art gallery visit

Please supply me with a written breakdown of the costs for the art gallery visit so that I can arrange for funding. How many staffing hours are involved?

You do not write 'Dear Madam' or 'Dear Sir' on a memo; they are quick and easy to send because you have said who the memo is to and who it is from in the heading.

? ACTIVITY

Write a memo from Jay Adams to Nagina Bibi telling her that the art gallery trip will cost £15 for petrol, and that you will need a driver and two care assistants for three hours each.

WRITING LETTERS

Care workers write formal letters to workers in other agencies. They may need to write to ask for information, or to arrange for a service to be provided, or to confirm an arrangement or appointment that has been made over the phone. They may sometimes need to help clients to write letters.

A formal letter could be set out like the following example.

Piper Green Nursery
Harper Road
Lingford
Merechester MO1 2LV

Educational Toys Ltd
Bray Industrial Estate
Morbury
Merechester MO7 3MJ

23 May 1994

Dear Sir/Madam,

Please send us a copy of your latest Toy and Resources Catalogue, and the current price lists.

We would also like to know whether you can arrange transport of any large items ordered.

Yours faithfully,

Jane Lang

Ms Jane Lang
Nursery Officer

Sometimes, if a word processor is used, both addresses and the date will appear on the left of the letter. Quite a lot of work places have special headed notepaper that has the name and the address of the facility on it, with a phone number and perhaps a fax number too.

If you know the name of the person you are writing to, you would use that instead of 'Sir/Madam', and if you use a person's name you should end with 'Yours sincerely' instead of 'Yours faithfully'.

As well as setting out the letter properly, it is important to write using sentences, paragraphs, and correct punctuation. This makes the letter clear, and easy for the person receiving it to understand. You usually need to plan a letter and make a draft before it is typed or word-processed. You should try to make your letter as brief and clear as possible.

?

ACTIVITY

Some students in Emma and Pete's group have written letters using the following information:

A letter to: Ms Janice Moore

       at: Oldbury Living Services Ltd
            Barrow Street
            Oldbury
            Merechester
            MO7 3LZ

to confirm that you will be visiting on 7 June 1994 at 2.15 pm with a party of ten students from Merechester College. You are interested in seeing what aids and special products are available to help people to manage independently in their own homes.

Look at the letters three students have written, and give each letter a mark out of 20. Remember to check that the letter is properly set out, whether it includes all the necessary information, and whether it is clear and easy to understand, using sentences, paragraphs and correct punctuation.

Letter 1

Central College
Merechester

Dear Madam

We are visiting on 7th June 1994 in the afternoon and there'll be ten students to see the aids and other things.

Yours sincerely,

Ann Walsh

Letter 2

Central College, Merechester
Oldfield Road
Merechester
MO7 3JS

Janice Moore
Oldbury Living Services Ltd
Barrow Street
Oldbury
Merechester
MO7 3LZ

Dear Ms Moore,

I will be visiting your establishment on 7th June 1994 at 2.15 p.m. with nine others from Central College. We are interested in the different aids and special products you have and hope to see as much as possible.

Yours sincerely

Phil Carnegie

Mr P. Carnegie

COMMENT

The first letter had an incomplete address for the college, no address for the people being written to, no date, no time for the visit, little information and used 'Dear Madam' with 'Yours sincerely' instead of 'Yours faithfully'. It would barely do to give the basic information needed. You might have given it 4 or 5 out of 20.

The second letter had the proper addresses, but no date. The salutation 'Dear Ms Moore' was accompanied with the appropriate closing phrase 'Yours sincerely'. The basic information was correct and reasonably clear and brief. This letter would be quite effective. You might have given it between 12 and 14 out of 20.

Letter 3

Central College, Merechester
Oldfield Road
Merechester
MO7 3JS
Tel: 373 2896

Janice Moore
Oldbury Living Services Ltd
Barrow Street
Oldbury
Merechester
MO7 3LZ

25th May 1994

Dear Ms Moore,

I am writing to confirm that a party of ten students will be visiting on 7th June 1994 at 2.15 p.m.

We are particularly interested in seeing what aids and special products are available to help people to manage independently in their own homes.

We are all care students who hope to work as carers, so we will find the knowledge we gain useful for our course and in our future jobs.

Yours sincerely,

Salma Khan

Ms S. Khan

The third letter included the college telephone mumber, which might be useful, and was dated. The necessary information was included, and some brief information about the interests and aims of the students was given. The whole letter was properly set out, with correct use of sentences, punctuation and paragraphs. You might have given it between 18 and 20 marks.

? ACTIVITY

Now practise writing a formal letter yourself. Imagine that you are a care assistant at:

Merryfield House
Langley Street
Limbury
L73 2IZ
Tel: 323 4921

You are writing to Mr Joe Bright at:

Limbury Library Services Dept
Limbury Council Offices
Brick Street
Limbury
L72 3ML

You want to invite Mr Bright to come and speak to your staff and resident group on 6 February at 2.30 pm about library services for people with visual impairments.

You have spoken to him on the telephone about this, and agreed a date, which you are now writing to confirm. There will be about six staff members and 22 residents present, and you hope Mr Bright will stay for tea at 4 pm.

LOG-BOOK ENTRIES

Some workplaces have log books for workers to record information that needs to be passed on to other workers. This can be particularly important in residential facilities where staff work in shifts and come on duty at different times.

The type of information recorded in the log book will vary, depending on the particular establishment's needs and procedures. Staff might record visits by the doctor or nurse and who was seen, information about arrangements that have been made or need to be made, arrivals of new residents, any important news or any incidents that occurred during the time the worker was on duty.

Log-book entries should be brief, clear and 'objective' – the opinions or feelings of the worker should not normally appear in the log book. Entries should give a date, time, and the name or initials of the worker who is writing.

An example of a log-book entry is given below.

Monday, 9th November

8–4 Shift, Joseph Makembe on duty

Plumber came at 9 am to do the work on the new kitchen. He's returning tomorrow to finish off. Says new kitchen should be ready for use by Wednesday. Paul Jenkins, new resident, arrived at 2 pm with social worker Mrs Allen. I've spoken with Paul and Mrs Allen, then showed Paul round again and introduced him to some of the other residents. He is in room 10, has his key and all his introductory information. I am his key worker, and I've arranged to see him again tomorrow evening after tea.

Michael Brown has told me that he's been offered an interview at Field Centre Workshops, Thursday 10 am. Suggest someone spends some time with him this evening to discuss this; he said he'd like some help to prepare.

John Sanders, social worker, rang to discuss referral of a client currently in emergency hostel accomodation. He is sending written information. Explained no vacancies at present, but as Simon Blake is due to move in to council flat next week we may soon have a place.

Spent some time with Simon this morning making a list of what he needs for his flat. He seems quite anxious about being there on his own. He and I plan to visit on Friday morning, to measure for curtains.

Jamie Kerr lit a sparkler (left over from 5th Nov) in the dining room this morning. I accompanied him into the garden with it, and talked at length about safety/fire risks. Suggest his key worker follows this up.

Bath plug's disappeared from bathroom 2. A prize to anyone who finds it this evening! Otherwise, we need to buy one tomorrow.

Petty cash checked and balanced.

The log book in this hostel is used to pass on information for the worker(s) who will be on the next shift. It also acts as a diary that can be looked back on if necessary. A lot of other things will have happened during the day, but the worker recorded what he felt were the important items. If he wrote everything down, there'd be too much to read, and it would take too much of his time. He has to be **selective**.

He also has to be **objective**, that is, not put in his feelings or opinions if he can avoid it. He did note that Simon Blake seemed anxious, though. The worker used his judgement here to record his opinion about Simon's state of mind.

? ## ACTIVITY

- If you are on work placement, try writing an objective log-book entry about a day at placement.

- If you are not on placement, you could try writing an objective account of a day at college.

REPORTS

Reports are written for various reasons in care workplaces. Sometimes an incident or emergency may have occurred which the person on duty writes a report about, to give a clear account of what happened and what action they took. Care establishments have legal responsibilities towards their clients, so a clear report of action taken in an emergency is important.

Reports should be written in a clear, straightforward way that is easy for the reader to understand. The writer should only include what they themselves witnessed or observed – they should not make guesses about what other people might have thought or done. If more than one worker is present during an incident or emergency, then each person can report about what they did or observed.

Here is an example of a report about an incident.

Incident Report

Theresa Kelly

On Thursday, 12th August I was on duty on the 4 pm–12 midnight shift. Just after 5 pm I went to the lounge to speak to Mr Lucas. As I approached I heard Mr Lucas calling for help. I entered the lounge, and found Mr Lucas attempting to assist Mrs Drew, who had fallen. As I entered I pressed the 'Emergency Call' button to alert other staff.

Mrs Drew had fallen with her left arm bent awkwardly under her. She was conscious and I asked her if she was alright. She said she had fallen on her arm and that her arm was hurting. She was not bleeding and I made no attempt to move her. I told Mr Lucas it was best not to move her, and said that help was on its way.

Just then, Peter Bell and Jean Devereaux (officer-in-charge) arrived and took over the care of Mrs Drew. Peter Bell asked me to assist Mr Lucas, who was pale and seemed shocked. I helped Mr Lucas to a seat, and spoke reassuringly to him. He asked to remain until Mrs Drew was taken to hospital, and I then made him a cup of tea and stayed with him for about 15 minutes when Jean Devereaux took over from me and asked me to return to my other duties.

? ACTIVITY

Imagine that you are one of the other workers mentioned in the above report – Peter Bell or Jean Devereaux. Write an objective report of this incident from their point of view.

GETTING IT WRITE

In all writing, it is important to use sentences, paragraphs and correct punctuation.

Sentences always start with a capital letter and end with a full stop. A sentence is a unit of writing that makes sense. These statements. Are not sentences. Because they. Do not make. Sense on their own.

A **paragraph** is made up of sentences that are about the same idea or point. Organising sentences into paragraphs helps to make the meaning of the writing clear. Each time you have a new idea or point to make, you should start a new paragraph. This also helps to divide up the text, so it is easier to read.

Writing is like speaking, with the reader as your 'listener'. When you speak, you use sentences, and you 'punctuate' your speech with pauses, gaps and changes of tone, so that your listener can understand what you are saying. When you write, you use punctuation instead, so that the reader can make sense of what you have written.

Full stops show that a sentence has ended. **Commas** are used when, if you were speaking, you would pause. You might use commas in a list, between each item, or to divide up a long sentence. **Question marks** are used to show that a question has been asked.

Apostrophes are used to show that part of a word has been left out, for example, didn't – did not, or we've – we have. Apostrophes are also used to show 'ownership' of something, for example, Mr Brett's room, or the warden's flat, or John's idea. When there is more than one owner, this is shown by putting the apostrophe after the 's', for example, the Bretts' room, or the residents' lounge, or the workers' reactions.

?

ACTIVITY

In the following passage, all the punctuation has been left out. Add capital letters, full stops, commas, question marks, and apostrophes where needed, to make sentences that are clear for the reader. Divide the passage into paragraphs each time there is a new idea, and to break up the text on the page.

why do care workers need to bother about punctuation or organising their writing care workers organise their writing and use punctuation because it helps to make what they write clear and easy to understand this can be very important if a care worker is writing in a log book or writing a report of an incident or emergency a workers actions in an emergency may need to be clearly explained use of sentences and paragraphs is important because it breaks up the text for the reader it can be quite off putting to see a big block of writing if there are no sentences or paragraphs it is likely that the reader will get confused about the writers meaning using sentences and paragraphs organises the meaning and ideas commas apostrophes full stops capital letters and question marks also help the reader to understand what the writer means care workers often write important letters or memos to make arrangements or order equipment needed for clients safety or well-being clients may ask care workers to help them with letter writing or to fill in forms.

GNVQ COMMUNICATION CORE SKILLS
LEVEL 1

Element 1.2   Produce written material

Performance criteria

You must be able to do the following things.

- Include information which is accurate and relevant to the subject.
- Check that text is legible and meaning is clear, correcting it if necessary.
- Follow appropriate standard conventions.
- Present information in a format that suits the audience and purpose.

Range

- **Subject**: straightforward.

- **Conventions**: spelling, punctuation, grammar.

- **Format**: pre-set, outline.

- **Audience**: people familiar with the subject who know you.

LEVEL 2

Element 2.2   Produce written material

Performance criteria

You must be able to do the following things.

- Include information which is accurate and relevant to the subject.
- Check that text is legible and meaning is clear, correcting it if necessary.
- Follow appropriate standard conventions.
- Present information in a format that suits the audience and purpose.
- Use structure and style to emphasise meaning.

Range

- **Subject matters**: straightforward.

- **Conventions**: spelling, punctuation, grammar.

- **Format**: pre-set, outline.

- **Audience**: people familiar with the subject who know you, people familiar with the subject who do not know you.

8 USING IMAGES TO COMMUNICATE IN CARE SETTINGS

This chapter looks at:

- **Using images in care settings**
- **Using tables**
- **Designing posters and notices**
- **Diagrams, graphs and charts**

WAYS OF USING IMAGES

Using images to communicate is very natural for most people. In fact, it is so natural we forget that we do it. Yet you could say that our eyes are a type of camera that photograph or film the world around us all the time. Even when we are not speaking or listening or using words, we are looking at the 'picture' of our surroundings. We are seeing colours and shapes and patterns that communicate meanings to us.

Look around the room you are in now. If there are people in it, you can learn things just from looking at them. If there are no people, you still get 'messages' – from the colours of the walls and floors, from the types and shapes of the furniture, from the decorations and ornaments, from the objects you can see in the room, from the things you can see out of the windows.

Babies first learn language through linking words with the people and things they see – mummy, daddy, baby, cat, etc. The first books babies look at are picture books, so they learn to link spoken words with images (pictures) of familiar things.

Try describing *everything* you can see around you now.

Give up?!

It takes a long time to describe in words what we can see. Pictures and images, therefore, are a very quick and powerful way of communicating a lot of information without using words.

Care workers use images in very many different ways. Workers with children use pictures and images to help children learn words and numbers, and encourage children to express their ideas and thoughts through painting, drawing, and making their own pictures. Art therapists help people to express themselves through images, too.

In medical settings, graphs or charts are often used to show information about people's health. Reminiscence work with elderly people often centres around old photographs and pictures of days gone by. Care workers in many settings use signs and posters to give information or advertise events.

Workers may help people, such as young anorexic people or children who have suffered abuse, to express events through pictures. Pictures may be used to help people with learning difficulties understand written information. Youth workers or play workers may help young people to decorate their surroundings with wall paintings.

Hospitals use scanners to see how a baby is developing, and parents are given a picture showing their baby in the mother's womb. Pictures and diagrams are used in pre-natal classes to show how the mother's body and the baby within will change and progress. These are just some of the uses of images in care settings.

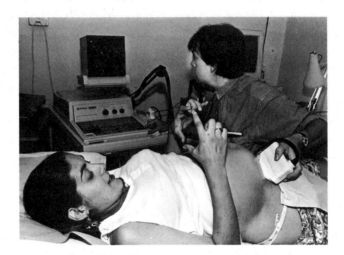

DESIGNING POSTERS AND NOTICES

Getting noticed

Care workers may want to make posters or notices for all sorts of reasons. They may want to advertise an activity, meeting or outing. They may want to remind people about something. They may want to use posters to educate people about health. Whatever the reason, it is certain that the poster or notice will be intended to catch people's attention. How eye-catching is this example?

Important Notice

We are having a meeting on Thursday at 3 pm to discuss activities.
Please come along – it's your youth club.

Not very eye-catching, is it?

? ACTIVITY

Can you suggest some ways to make this notice more likely to catch the attention of youth club members?

! COMMENT

First, the notice would need to be larger. Colours could be used. A more interesting and eye-catching title could be thought of. Size of lettering could be varied. Most important, a picture or pictures could be added.

There are different ways of catching people's attention: use of colour, pictures, size of poster, size of titles and words, bold writing, humour, 'shock' tactics, layout (the way words and pictures are placed and spaced out) and text (the writing) all play a part.

One way of learning about these ways of catching attention is to look at adverts on hoardings or in newspapers and magazines. Advertisers are trying to sell products, so catching people's attention is important.

? ACTIVITY

Collect some adverts from newspapers or magazines. Try to see how the advertiser has used some of the ways listed above to catch people's attention.

Audience

As well as catching attention, it is important to think about *who* in particular you are aiming your notice or poster at. Who is your **audience**? A poster to interest young children would need to be different from a poster aimed at youth club members, for example. A poster advertising an activity for people in a day centre for elderly people would be different from a poster advertising a trip for parents and children in a nursery.

You can see this by thinking about advertisements. Adverts are directed at the person who might *buy* the product – so an advert for children's clothes, for example, might be directed at parents and/or grandparents and possibly angled towards women.

This might be done by using photographs of cute-looking children who seem happy and carefree, and are playing 'nicely' with each other, perhaps with some expensive toys. Pictures of pleased-looking parents or grandparents might be included. The advert might explain that the clothes are easy to wash, to appeal to busy parents.

The poster or notice you design will need to be different depending on *whose* attention you are trying to catch.

? ACTIVITY

- Use the adverts you have collected to think about the idea of different audiences.

- Who do you think the advert is aimed at?

- How has each advertiser made their advert appealing to the audience group who might buy the product?

? ACTIVITY

- Imagine you are a voluntary worker in a community centre. Two trips to the seaside are being planned. One is for youth club members, the other is for elderly people.

- What types of images/pictures would you use for each of these different audiences?

Clarity and relevance

The 'message' you are trying to communicate through your poster or notice needs to be **clear** and **relevant**. The illustrations, text and layout all contribute to this.

Relevance means that the picture or text must have something to do with the subject of the poster or notice. Imagine you were designing a health education poster aimed to encourage young people to avoid smoking during pregnancy. You would be unlikely to choose a picture of an elderly person in a wheelchair to illustrate it. You might choose a picture of a pregnant woman looking anxious.

You would be likely to use text that linked the idea of smoking to harmful effects on the foetus in the womb, rather than just a general slogan such as 'smoking kills'.

You would probably put the text and illustrations together in a way that might catch the attention of young parents, and that would show both image and text clearly, spacing things out rather than squashing in lots of writing that looked muddled.

? ACTIVITY

- Imagine that you are designing a health education poster to encourage young people to use condoms to avoid risks of contracting HIV through unprotected sex.

- What type of images or picture might you use? What text would you write? How would you design the layout?

- Make a rough design of your poster, and explain briefly why it is clear and relevant for its audience.

! COMMENT

In posters and notices, it is best to keep the text simple, and not to over-fill the space with too many words or images. If you over-fill it, it will look confusing and the 'message' will be less clear.

On the other hand, make sure all the necessary information has been included – times, dates and places of meetings or activities should be shown clearly, a person or place to contact for more information might be given.

Framing

Notices and posters can look much more effective if you add a frame or border. The simplest type of frame is a box (drawn with a ruler!) around the whole notice. You might design a more complicated border if you have more time and it seems suitable. You can also 'frame' or box-in *parts* of your text, such as the time/place/date of the event.

In some workplaces, computers may be available to help you design notices or posters. A variety of borders, text and graphics can be available on different software, to help you achieve a professional-looking result.

? ACTIVITY

Shown opposite are some notices that Emma and Pete's class designed. Try marking each notice out of 20, considering their effectiveness in catching attention, their suitability for their intended audience, the clarity and relevance of their content, and the style and simplicity of their overall design.

! COMMENT

Notice 1

This notice is not very eye-catching, because it is not very clear. The 'bubble writing' is hard to read, and gets less clear at a distance. The pictures are not very relevant. There is no frame. The student has forgotten to check the spelling of 'residential'.

Important information has been included, but no date or time for the meeting is given. The style in not ideal for a student audience. Colours would liven it up, but might also make it more difficult to read.

You might have given this about 5 out of 20.

Notice 2

This notice has a frame, and catches the eye because of the large 'DON'T' and 'OK'. Using stencils can make a notice look second rate, but here they seem appropriate, although they could have been used more evenly. The message is clear, with some humour that is suitable for the audience of students it is aimed at. The place, time and date of the event are given. Though it looks as if it was done a bit quickly, this is quite an effective notice – you might have given it around 12 out of 20.

Notice 3

This notice was made using a computer. The border is well-suited to the subject, and looks interesting. The message is simple and clear.

It was aimed at parents or others who might park in front of the nursery when dropping off children, and would be an effective sign. It is not over-crowded with graphics or images that might make the important words less clear. You might have given this notice around 16 to 18 out of 20.

DIAGRAMS, TABLES, GRAPHS AND CHARTS

Diagrams

One type of diagram used in care settings is a **life-map**, or life-line. This may be used to help a client think back over their life and remember important events that may have affected their development. Young people with problems, such as anorexia, or people with alcohol problems, may be

Notice 1

important meeting
for
HEALTH and
SOCIAL CARE
STUDENTS

—TO PLAN FOR THE
RESIDENTIEL

in Room 61
on wednesday !

Notice 3

Please

DON'T PARK

in front of the

nursery

Notice 2

DON'T

miSS The end of terM Disco

O K ?

ROOM 12   FRIDAY 17th JULY 7:30

encouraged to draw a life-map to discuss with a care worker or therapist, to increase the person's self-awareness. Life-maps help people to understand different events, people and environments that have influenced them.

Drawing a life-map involves the person imagining their life as a line or road that begins with birth (or conception) and is drawn as a progressing route showing events, such as childhood illnesses or special achievements, starting new schools, gaining qualifications, family deaths or bereavements, personal difficulties, or particular successes, along the way.

Pictures or symbols of people or events can be included, and the road may be shown as going 'up' or 'down', twisting or turning, as seems appropriate to the person drawing it. The life-map can help a person think about their life.

?   ## ACTIVITY

Try drawing a 'map' of your own life, marking events that were/are important to you along the route. This can be a useful activity for increasing self-awareness.

Tables, graphs and charts

Tables, graphs and charts offer ways of summing up information that would take a long time to write out in words. One form of table that you may often use is a bus timetable. Imagine how complicated it would look if all the bus times were written out in words!

Many of the tables and charts of information that provide useful knowledge for care workers are easier to read than bus timetables.

Care workers may want to use tables to help them, or their clients, work out nutritional values of foods. The following two tables are part of the nutritional information given on packets of breakfast cereal.

Breakfast cereal I	
Nutritional information	per 100 g
Energy	422 kcal
Protein	8.5 g
Carbohydrates	62 g
(of which sugars)	25 g
Fat	16 g
(of which saturates)	6 g
Fibre	8 g
Sodium	0.5 g

Breakfast cereal 2	
Nutritional information	per 100 g
Energy	380 kcal
Protein	5 g
Carbohydrate	87 g
(of which sugars)	40 g
Fat	1 g
(of which saturates)	0.5 g
Fibre	1 g
Sodium	0.8 g

? ACTIVITY

- Which cereal is higher in fibre?

- Which cereal is lower in fat?

- Would either of these cereals be ideal for someone who needed a high-fibre, low-fat diet?

- Look at nutritional tables on cereal packets next time you are at the shops to find one that is both high in fibre and low in fat.

Carers working with babies often come across useful information in tables and charts.

Weaning chart

Baby's age	Suitable foods
3–4 months	Baby rice cereals, mixed with breast milk or formula milk. Fresh fruit, cooked and puréed. Root vegetables, cooked and puréed.
4–6 months	Lean chicken, white fish (purée these using a blender).
6–8 months	Baby cereal, citrus fruits, pasta, lean meat (food may be mashed rather than puréed, and mixtures such as cereal and fruit can be introduced).
Over 8 months	Raw carrots, celery, and finger foods, pulses such as lentils and split peas, liver and oily fish, berry fruits.

Do not add salt or sugar to your baby's foods.

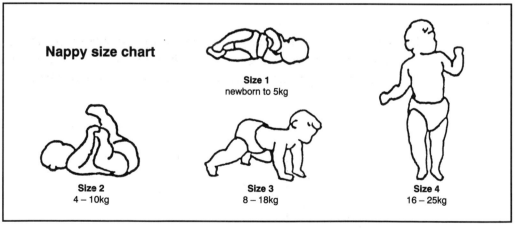

Nappy size chart

Size 1
newborn to 5kg

Size 2
4 – 10kg

Size 3
8 – 18kg

Size 4
16 – 25kg

? ACTIVITY

Using the weaning chart, answer the following questions:

- What foods can be introduced to babies at 4–6 months?
- How may foods be prepared for babies at 6–8 months?

Using the nappy size chart, answer the following questions:

- What size nappy is suitable for a baby weighing 7 kg?
- What size nappy is suitable for a baby weighing 19 kg?

Bar charts are usually used to compare different categories, or to compare figures from different regions or countries. This bar chart compares reasons for children being on the child protection register.

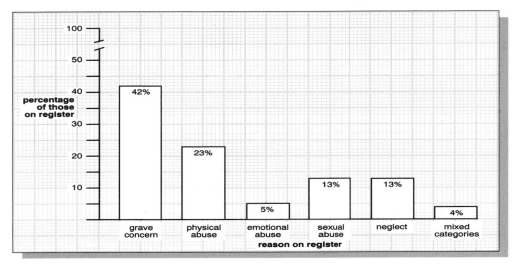

Children on the Child Protection Register by reason, 1990 (England and Wales)
Source: Department of Health, Welsh Office

Line graphs are used to show changes in figures over a period of time. A centile chart, which shows the average weight gain of a baby, is a type of line graph. This line graph shows deaths in fires from 1971 to 1989.

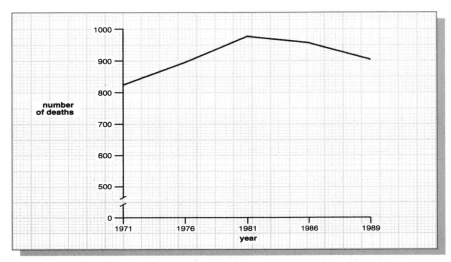

Fatal casualities in fires (UK)
Source: Home Office

Pie charts are used to show how a particular figure is divided up between different categories. This pie chart shows the way people divide up into households of different sizes.

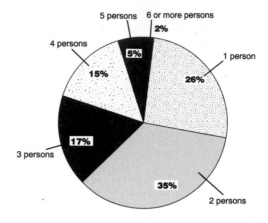

Household size 1990–91 (Great Britain)
Source: Office of Population Censuses and Surveys

? ACTIVITY

On the following graphs and charts, some information needs to be added. See if you can fit the information on to the graph or chart in the place where it is supposed to go.

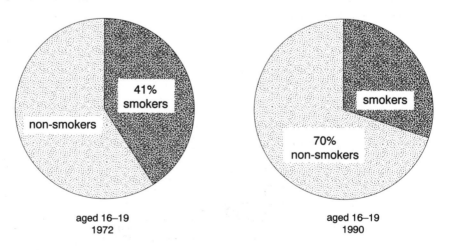

Cigarette smokers in the 16–19 age group (Great Britain)
Source: General Household Survey

In 1972 41% of the 16–19 age group were smokers. In 1990 the figure had dropped to 30%. Label the pie charts with the missing percentages.

Add a line to this graph to show women's life expectation.

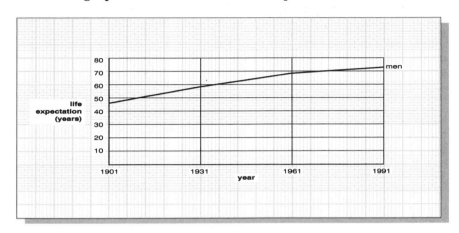

Life expectation (UK)
Source: Government Actuary's Department

Life expectation

Men	*Age*	*Women*	*Age*
1901	46	1901	49
1931	58	1931	62
1961	68	1961	74
1991	73	1991	79

Add the other four bars to this chart, using the information on household type given overleaf.

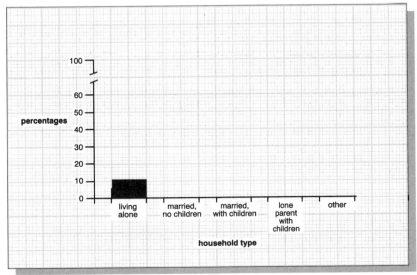

People in households 1990–91 (Great Britain)
Source: Office of Population Censuses and Surveys

Household type

Living alone	11%
Married, no children	24%
Married with children	51%
Lone parent with children	6%
Other	8%

GNVQ COMMUNICATION CORE SKILLS
LEVEL 1

Element 1.3   Use images

Performance criteria

You must be able to do the following things.

- Select images which clearly illustrate the points being made.
- Use images which are suited to the audience, situation and purpose.
- Use images at appropriate times and places.

Range

- **Images**: taken from others' material, produced by you.

- **Points**: on straightforward subjects.

- **Audience**: people familiar with the subject who know you.

- **Situation:** in written material, in one-to-one discussions, in group discussions.

LEVEL 2

Element 2.3   Use images

Performance criteria

You must be able to do the following things.

- Select images which clearly illustrate the points being made.
- Use images which are suited to the audience, situation and purpose.
- Use images at appropriate times and places.

Range

- **Images**: taken from others' material, produced by you.

- **Points**: on straightforward subjects.

- **Audience**: people familiar with the subject who know you, people familiar with the subject who do not know you.

- **Situation:** in written material, in one-to-one discussions, in group discussions.

READING AND RESPONDING TO INFORMATION IN CARE SETTINGS

This chapter looks at

- **Identifying the main points in:**
  memos
  letters
  log-book entries
  dialogue
  factual information
  graphs

- **Defining words and terms**

Care workers need to be able to read, understand, and respond to written information. They need to be able to pick out the important points from the material they are reading or looking at. When they are skilled at doing this, they are able to reply to memos and letters quickly, or take action on messages in log books, reports or correspondence.

Most people come across words or phrases that they do not understand when they are reading. Sometimes we might just skip a word that is unfamiliar or difficult, and try to get the general sense of what we are reading. This can be a good tactic for a first reading, but it may cause us problems to continually skip unfamiliar words.

In care work, words and terms that are unfamiliar to the new worker will come up from time to time in memos, forms, reports, letters and other material. To be sure that they have understood fully, the worker will have to find out what those unfamiliar words or terms mean. One way of doing this would be to look up the word in a dictionary, so it is useful to have a dictionary to hand.

Dictionaries do not always give the meanings of specialist words, or terms, though. Another way of finding out the meaning of an unfamiliar term would be to ask an experienced worker or supervisor to explain it. If you do this, make a note of the word or term and its meaning, and keep your notes together in a file or notebook. You will soon build up a useful dictionary of

specialist terms, and you will not have to keep asking if you forget what the word means.

If you are dealing with a lot of specialist terms, you may find that there is a book or manual in the workplace to help you understand the terms – ask your supervisor about this.

MEMOS AND LETTERS

In order to reply to a memo or letter, or to take action on it, a care worker has to know what the **main points** made in the memo or letter are. Memos are often quite short, so there is usually not too much to read through in order to work out how to reply to, or act on, the message.

? ACTIVITY

- What is the subject of the following memo?
- There are five main points in the memo – briefly list what they are.

Memo

To: Lynn (care assistant)   **From:** Joan Henderson (officer-in-charge)

Date: 12 October 1994   **Subject:** Leisure centre use/access

The new leisure centre's opened at Banks Road. I'd like you to visit the leisure centre and check on the following:

Wheelchair access to sports facilities – there's a ramp to the main entrance, but could you check out access to the different sports facilities and changing rooms.

Wheelchair access to other areas – find out what the access is like to spectator areas, and the cafeteria and toilets.

Pick up leaflets and information about facilities, times, costs, etc. – get a few copies of everything so we can have some on display and some for reference.

COMMENT

- The subject of the memo is leisure centre use and access.
- The five main points are:

    (1) The new leisure centre has opened.

    (2) The care assistant is asked to visit the leisure centre.

    (3) She is asked to find out about wheelchair access to sports facilities.

    (4) She is asked to find out about wheelchair access to other areas.

    (5) She is asked to pick up copies of leaflets and information.

Notice that a **main point** appeared in each paragraph of the memo. You will often find that this is the case when reading memos, letters and reports – a new paragraph usually deals with a new point.

ACTIVITY

- What is the main subject of the following letter?
- What are the main points made in the letter?

Beaconsfield Trust Farm Museum
Oak Grange, Cradlebridge
Beaconsfield BL7 2JB

Sara Grey
Bell Road Nursery, 15–17 Bell Road
Pridford, Branchester BH2 1LB

27 May 1994

Dear Ms Grey,

Thank you for your enquiry about visits to the Beaconsfield Trust Farm Museum.

The farm museum welcomes group visits, and there is good access to the farm and facilities for pushchairs. There are ground floor toilets with baby changing facilities.

The restaurant dining area is on the ground floor, and we supply high-chairs, children's meals and baby foods, as well as a full range of lunches, teas, snacks and drinks.

There is an enclosed area where small children can see rabbits, sheep and lambs, goats and kids, hens, ducks, geese and donkeys. This area includes a fenced pond. Animals are fed at specified times, and children often enjoy joining in with this activity.

There are various indoor displays at the farm, and I enclose leaflets describing these. Children and adults can look at and handle farm equipment, and there is a video about lambing time.

I enclose a leaflet giving our opening times and admission costs that includes details of discounts. If you would like to book a visit, please fill in and return the booking form.

I hope to hear from you soon.

Yours sincerely,

Bronwen Davis

Education Officer
Beaconsfield Trust Farm Museum

! **COMMENT**

- The subject of the letter is Beaconsfield Trust Farm Museum.

- The main points are:

  (1) There is access to suitable facilities for babies and small children.

  (2) There are refreshment facilities for adults, children, and babies.

  (3) There is a safe area for small children to see and feed farm animals.

  (4) There are indoor displays.

  (5) A leaflet is enclosed giving opening times and costs.

  (6) Visits should be booked in advance.

Again, you probably noticed that each paragraph of the letter from Beaconsfield Trust Farm Museum made a different point.

Selecting the main points is a way of 'summing up' the information. It can be useful to do this before you reply to a memo or letter. In time, you will find that the skill becomes automatic.

? **ACTIVITY**

The following log-book entry is not as clear as it could be. Try rewriting the entry, cutting out unnecessary details and keeping the main points of the information.

Log book

Tuesday Daytime shift – Jane Bray and Marie Caprielli

Very busy this morning, the phone never stopped ringing and we were so rushed off our feet going back and forth to the office, that I felt like unplugging it!

Visit from Mrs Jones, social worker, to see Mr Allen about his move to sheltered accommodation. Mrs Jones stayed for about an hour and had tea and biscuits. She hasn't been here before, she said she found it interesting. She will be visiting again on Friday to collect Mr Allen to go to look at his flat – he's very pleased about it all, although there's a lot of things to sort out and he's a bit worried about being so far away from his daughter, but she's got a car, so it should be alright.

Mrs Jenkins tells me there's a bulb gone on the top landing which better be sorted out because it could be a hazard if left in darkness. I've mentioned it to John and he is going to sort it out this afternoon if possible.

Mrs McColl and her daughter came to look around, and stayed for lunch. Mrs McColl is moving in next week, she had a good look around and was introduced to people. She says she likes the garden, it was looking nice in the sunshine, and she will need a ground floor room.

There's a problem in the laundry room, one of the machines is flooding. I've rung the plumber who can't come today, so that machine is out of use, but he will call tomorrow at 2 pm and will probably sort it out then. I had to put all the washing in the other machine, but it's sorted out now. There was a lot of mopping up to do, too.

Mrs Lane visited from the community centre to say that they are running a new art and craft afternoon on Wednesdays, she thought some residents would be interested. She has put up a poster on the notice board and asked us to remind people about it. It sounds as if it will be an enjoyable class, they've got a tutor from the college coming in, and there's quite a variety of activities. Mrs Lane says she'll be in again on Friday to chat to people about it.

Mrs Brett and Mrs Carlson went to out-patients today for their appointments – they will be back about 5 pm and Mrs Brett's daughter phoned to say she will arrive at 6 pm, but I couldn't pass on the message because her Mum was already gone, so please mention it to her when she returns.

Now take a look at this discussion between Emma and Pete.

Emma and Pete

Emma was thinking about what she wanted to do next year.

'What have you decided, Pete?' she asked.

'GNVQ Advanced. We're still too young for most jobs, and anyway, I might end up going to University, you never know ...'

Emma frowned. 'I *need* money. I've got a job at the chemist's over the summer. I was going to do the Diploma in Nursery Nursing in September ... I've been offered a place.'

'But?' prompted Pete.

'But ... I don't know. I'm not so sure I want to work in a nursery anymore ... The Adult Training Centre's really interesting, and they're so busy ... I'm still doing voluntary work there.'

'Is that the sort of work you really want to do?' asked Pete. 'Phil says he was really tired the whole time he was there; he likes the play group much better.'

'Well, that's just Phil – he's always on his feet in the play group, he does all sorts of stuff with the kids – but he doesn't think of it as work.' Emma smiled. 'That's how I feel about the Training Centre. I think I'd like to work with people with learning difficulties.'

She drummed her fingers on the desk, and looked puzzled. 'Salma's doing Health Studies. She wants to do nursing. Alan's going on an Access course. Amanda's got a job with elderly people ... Everyone knows what they're doing except me!'

'Have you seen the Careers Officer?' asked Pete.

'Twice. She gave me lots of information. But I'm still not sure. There are lots of jobs in nurseries ...'

'What does your mum say?' asked Pete.

Emma grinned. 'Oh, she's really pleased I'm staying on at college. She keeps saying how lucky I am. She wanted to do art when she was younger but her dad said she had to do typing and get a job.'

Pete nodded. 'My dad's getting less worried about me doing care. He used to keep on about it, how you couldn't get anywhere in care work, not a career for a family man and so on. But he didn't really know about any of the jobs there are. I've been telling him what the Careers Officer said, showing him leaflets and the college course books. He's calmed down a bit now.'

Emma smiled, 'I bet he's impressed with your Distinction grade on the Portfolio!'

Pete smiled modestly. 'Well, yes ...' He looked sympathetically at Emma.

'What are you going to do, then?'

Emma shrugged. 'I think I'll go and talk to Mrs Brent. Again. And the Childcare tutor. It's two years of my life, so I'd better make sure I choose the course I want.'

Later she met Pete in the canteen.

'How did it go?' he asked.

'Well, I think I've decided.' Emma announced, looking pleased. 'I spoke to everyone again, and I'm going to do the Advanced Level. Mrs Brent gave me a book on different jobs with people with learning difficulties.' Emma showed the book to Pete. 'There's units on Special Needs and Special Communication Skills on the Advanced, and she said I could try out different placements in that type of work. She kept saying, "It's a broad qualification, Emma, you don't have to decide on your career finally yet, there are *lots* of options open to you!" So that's taken the pressure off, really – and I'm looking forward to next year!'

? ACTIVITY

- Sum up the main points in this discussion between Emma and Pete.

- Write your summary in the **past tense**, for example, Pete said he was going to do the GNVQ Advanced Level; Emma said she was thinking of doing a childcare course, etc.

? ACTIVITY

- Read the following information about sugar and its effects on teeth, and look at the diagram.

- Design a leaflet or poster that sums up the main points of the information – you might use some pictures or graphics to get these points across.

SUGAR

Sugar contains no fibre, protein, or vitamins. Yet each person in the UK consumes an average of 88 lb of sugar a year! Apart from sugar that we add to drinks and foods, sugar is included in many products we buy, such as pickles, jams, honey, syrup and confectionery. 'Natural' sugar occurs in fruit drinks, too, and in products we may think of as 'healthy', such as some yoghurts, mueslies, and dried fruits.

Sugar can cause tooth decay. This can start when children or babies are given dummies that have been dipped in fruit juices or sweet drinks. Even some medicines contain sugar. Bacteria that is naturally present in teeth can form acid when sugar is eaten. This can then cause dental caries (tooth decay).

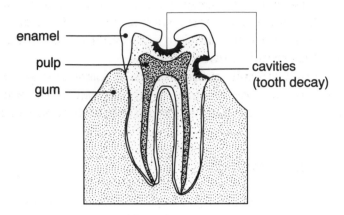

Research has shown that acid in plaque can be formed even with amounts of sugar that cannot be tasted. Sugar eaten with other foods at mealtimes is less likely to cause decay than eating sweet foods or having sugary drinks between meals. Sweets tend to cause more problems because they are in the mouth for longer.

Experiments with volunteers have shown that people who did not brush their teeth, and who rinsed with sugar every two hours would tend to develop decay within three weeks. Those who did *not* brush their teeth, but also did *not* have the sugar rinses, did *not* get this quick decaying effect. However, brushing thoroughly with a fluoride toothpaste is recommended, as it also helps prevent periodontal diseases – diseases that affect the gums and bones supporting the teeth.

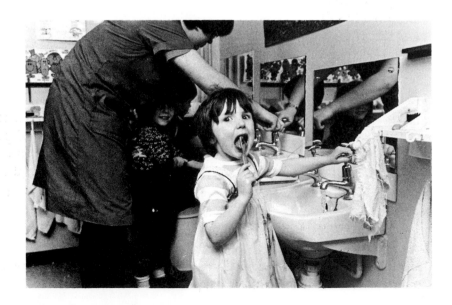

Snacks that are healthy alternatives to sugary foods include fresh fruits and raw vegetables, such as carrots. Fizzy drinks can be high in sugar, though low-calorie drinks can also be acidic. Tea, coffee, or milk are best drunk unsweetened.

Look carefully at food labels, as forms of sugar occur in many foods. Glucose, sucrose, fructose, dextrose, and lactose are words which you might not immediately recognise, but which are all forms of sugar.

DEFINING WORDS

You can use dictionaries to find the meanings of words. You can also use specialist books about the subject. Using the **contents** page at the front of a book will help you find out what topics are covered in each chapter. The **index** at the back of a book, in alphabetical order, tells you what page numbers look up to find the word you are interested in. Some books also have a **glossary** which gives the meanings of specialist words.

? ACTIVITY

- Use the contents and index of this book (which gives page references for each word or item) and a dictionary to find the meaning of the following words or terms. Write a couple of sentences to define each term.

  Confidentiality
  Discrimination
  Empowerment
  Eye contact
  Individuality
  Prompts
  Self-esteem
  Stereotyping
  Tone of voice

- You could use these definitions as the start of a glossary or dictionary of your own. Use a loose-leaf file or notebook, allowing several pages for each letter of the alphabet, so that you can add new words as you come across them. You might want to add pictures to illustrate some of these terms.

TABLES, GRAPHS AND DIAGRAMS

Tables, graphs and diagrams illustrate information, and a care worker needs to be able to select the important points from these.

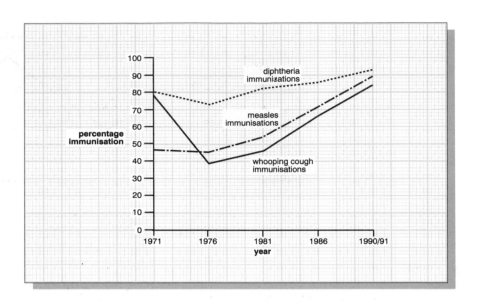

Immunisation of Children (UK)
Source: Health Departments and Services, England, Wales, Scotland and Northern Ireland

This graph shows the percentages of children who were immunised against diphtheria, whooping cough, and measles between 1971 and 1990–91.

You can see that the number of children immunised against diphtheria has risen from **80%** in 1971 to **93%** in 1990–91. There was a slight fall between 1971 and 1976.

Children immunised against measles has risen also, from **46%** in 1971 to **54%** in 1981, then sharply rising to **89%** in 1990–91.

Whooping cough immunisation, on the other hand, *fell* sharply from **78%** in 1971 to **39%** in 1976. (This was due to fears about the effects of whooping cough immunisation.) But by 1990–91, whooping cough immunisation had *risen* to **84%**.

The pollen count

Pollen grains are produced by grasses, trees and flowers mainly in spring and summer. The pollen count is the amount of pollen in the air at a certain time. People allergic or sensitive to pollen may get hay fever. It is useful for them to know when the pollen count is likely to be high. The pollen count varies from region to region and depending on the weather. Areas with more plants and trees have a higher pollen count. On cloudy or wet days the pollen count is likely to be lower than on warm, dry days.

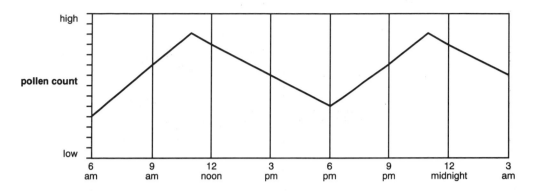

Pollen count changes during a warm, dry day (approximation)

? ACTIVITY

Using information from the graph and text, explain:

* the factors which are likely to result in a high pollen count;

* how the pollen count varies on warm, dry days.

? ACTIVITY

Describe the main points of information you notice in the following graph.

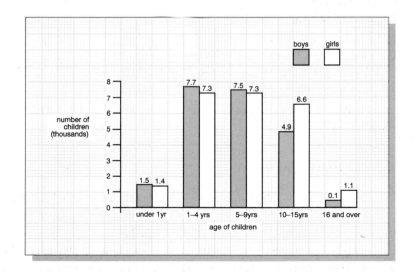

Children and young persons on the Child Protection Registers 1990 (England and Wales)
Source: Department of Health, Welsh Office

GNVQ COMMUNICATION CORE SKILLS
LEVEL 1

Element 1.4 *Read and respond to written materials*

Performance criteria

You must be able to do the following things.

- Read materials for a purpose.
- Extract the necessary information for a purpose.
- Use appropriate sources of reference to clarify understanding of the subject.

Range

- **Materials**: text, text supported by images, images supported by text.

- **Purpose**: to obtain information.

- **Sources of reference**: provided for you; written, oral.

- **Subject**: straightforward.

LEVEL 2

Element 2.4 *Read and respond to written materials*

Performance criteria

You must be able to do the following things.

- Select and read materials for a purpose.
- Extract the necessary information for a purpose.
- Use appropriate sources of reference to clarify understanding of the subject.
- Summarise the information extracted.

Range

- **Materials**: text, text supported by images, images supported by text.

- **Purpose**: to obtain information.

- **Sources of reference**: provided for you; written, oral.
- **Subject**: straightforward.
- **Summarise information:** in writing, orally.

FURTHER INFORMATION

In schools and colleges, students work towards the GNVQ (General National Vocational Qualification) in Health and Social Care. In care workplaces, staff can work towards the NVQ (National Vocational Qualification) in Care.

The NVQ in Care at Level 2 involves workers showing evidence of their skills relating to six core units. Workers also take some specialist units, in order to achieve full accreditation at NVQ Level 2.

The core units in Care at NVQ Level 2 are:

- Unit O: Promote equality for all individuals.
- Unit Z1: Contribute to the protection of individuals from abuse.
- Unit W2: Contribute to the ongoing support of clients and others significant to them.
- Unit W3: Support clients in transition due to their care requirements.
- Unit U4: Contribute to the health, safety and security of individuals and their environment.
- Unit U5: Obtain, transmit and store information relating to the delivery of a care service.

To gain the full NVQ at Level 2, workers also gain units that are relevant to the particular type of care work they do. These are called **endorsements**, and are available to workers in the following areas:

- Developmental Care
- Direct Care
- Domiciliary Support
- Residential/Hospital Support
- Post-natal Care
- Special Needs Care

There are a total of 15 units apart from the core units. Workers in different types of care work take between four and six of these; this then qualifies them at NVQ Level 2 in that area of work. If they moved to a *different* area of care work, they would have to gain any units they had not yet taken that are required for that area, in order to be qualified at NVQ Level 2 in their new job.

One of the NVQ core units, the 'O' unit, is the **value-base** unit. This unit is about principles of good practice in care. The value-base unit is understood as underpinning, and being part of, *all* the other units. This means that a worker has to show evidence of good practice relating to the value-base unit in *all* areas of work in which they are assessed.

The value-base unit is divided into five Elements. These are:

- Oa: Promote anti-discriminatory practice.
- Ob: Maintain confidentiality of information.
- Oc: Promote and support individual rights and choice within service delivery.
- Od: Acknowledge individuals' personal beliefs and identity.
- Oe: Support individuals through effective communication.

As you can see from the titles of the Elements, the principles of good practice set out in the NVQ value-base unit also relate to the GNVQ units in Health and Social Care; all these principles can be maintained in the way that you communicate and provide support, for example.

The GNVQ Intermediate Health and Social Care Unit 4, Communication and Interpersonal Relationships, is particularly relevant to these principles because it is skill-based, that is, you have to show that you can **do** things, as well as that you understand the **theory** of how to do them.

To gain an NVQ in Care, you have to both understand the ideas and knowledge behind the skills *and* show that you have those skills in care-work settings.

The GNVQ Communication Core Skills relate to the Care value-base unit, particularly to Element e: Support individuals through effective communication. This element mainly relates to face-to-face communication, with service users and others.

A further NVQ Level 2 core unit that relates to GNVQ Communication Core Skills is Unit U5: Obtain, transmit and store information relating to the delivery of a care service.

The Elements in this unit are:

- Obtain information relating to care service delivery.
- Maintain, store and retrieve records.
- Receive and transmit information to others on request.

As well as other skills, this NVQ core unit requires the worker to be able to deal appropriately and effectively with information in care settings, using written, face-to-face and electronic or telephone methods.

NVQs are assessed in the care workplace. Care-work supervisors are trained to assess workers. The workers gather evidence of their skills through showing examples of their recording, letter-writing, etc, through testimony of others, such as clients and other workers, through being observed by the assessor or others whilst working, and through being able to explain and answer questions about their work practice, and the knowledge that relates to it. They do not have to take any exams.

There are also NVQs at Level 2 available in Child Care and Education. For these there are eight core units, and workers in different childcare settings take additional specialist units. As in Care, these are called endorsement units.

The core units for the NVQ Level 2 in Child Care and Education are:

- Care for children's physical needs.
- Support children's social and emotional development.
- Contribute to the management of children.
- Set out and clear away play activities.
- Work with young children.
- Maintain a child-oriented environment.
- Maintain the safety of children.
- Establish and maintain relationships with parents of young children.

Endorsement units are available in the following child-work areas:

- Work with babies.
- Work in support of others.
- Work in a pre-school group.
- Work in a community-run pre-school group.

Workers can go on from Level 2 to Levels 3 and 4 in the NVQ framework. There are NVQs at Level 3 in Care, and in Child Care and Education. There are NVQs in Play work, starting at level 2, which are suited to workers in facilities such as adventure playgrounds and play centres. There are also NVQ awards at Levels 3 and 4 in the Criminal Justice Services, suitable for people working in facilities such as probation hostels and residential services for ex-offenders.

The National Council for Vocational Qualifications has responsibility for both GNVQs and NVQs.

The Central Council for Education and Training in Social Work (CCETSW) works together with City and Guilds as a Joint Awarding Body for NVQs in Care, Child Care and Education, and the Criminal Justice Services. The Business and Technology Education Council (BTEC) is also an awarding body for NVQs in Care. The Council for Awards in Childcare and Education (CACHE) awards NVQs in Child Care and Education.

GNVQ awards in Health and Social Care are available for people over 16, in some schools and in colleges at Foundation, Intermediate and Advanced levels, from BTEC, City and Guilds and RSA.

BIBLIOGRAPHY

Argyle, M. (1983), *The Psychology of Interpersonal Behaviour*, 4th edn, London: Penguin.

Bornat, J., Pereira, C., Pilgrim, D. and Williams, F. (Eds) (1993) *Community Care: A Reader*, London: Macmillan.

Brahan, P., Rattansi, A. and Skellington, R. (Eds) (1992) *Racism and Antiracism*, London: Sage.

Brain, J. and Martin, M. (1980), *Childcare and Health for Nursery Nurses*, Cheltenham: Stanley Thornes.

Burnard, P. (1992), *Communicate!*, London: Edward Arnold.

Burton, G. and Dimbleby, R. (1988), *Between Ourselves*, London: Edward Arnold.

Burton, G. and Dimbleby, R. (1986), *More Than Words*, London: Methuen.

Burton, G. and Dimbleby, R. (1990), *Teaching Communication*, London: Routledge.

Burton, G. (1990), *More than Meets the Eye: an Introduction to Media Studies*, London: Edward Arnold.

Darnborough, A. and Kinrade, D. (1991) *Directory for Disabled People*, Hemel Hempstead: Woodhead-Faulkner (in asociation with RADAR).

Douglas, T. (1976), *Groupwork Practice*, London: Tavistock Publications.

Fontana, D. (1990), *Social Skills at Work*, London: BPS Books, Routledge.

Hopson, B. and Scally, M. (1981), *Lifeskills Teaching*, Maidenhead: McGraw-Hill Book Co.

Johnson, D. and Johnson, F. (1975) Joining Together – *Group Theory and Group Skills*, London: Prentice-Hall.

Johnson, K. (1989), *Trauma in the lives of children*, London: Macmillan.

Levine, R. S., *The Scientific Basis of Dental Health Education* (pamphlet), Health Education Authority.

Maslow, A. (1954), *Motivation and personality*, New York: Harper & Row.

Meteyard, B. (1990), *Community Care Keyworker Manual*, London: Longman.

O'Connor, J. and Seymour, J. (1990) *Introducing Neurolinguistic Programming*, London: Harper Collins.

Priestly, P., McQuire, J., Flegg, D., Helmsley, V. and Welham, D. (1978), *Social Skills and Personal Problem Solving*, London: Tavistock.

Stewart, I. and Joinnes, V. (1987), *T A Today*, Nottingham: Lifespace.

Stoyle, J. (1991), *Caring for Older People: a Multi-cultural Approach*, Cheltenham: Stanley Thornes.

Thomson, H., Holder, C., Hutt, G., Meffitt, C., and Manuel J. (1994), *Health and Social Care for Advanced GNVQ*, London: Hodder and Stoughton.
Wadham, J. (1994), *Your Rights – The Library Guide*, 5th edn, London: Pluto Press (in association with the National Council for Civil Liberties.

3